Life Class

Life Class

THOUGHTS, EXERCISES,
REFLECTIONS
OF AN ITINERANT VIOLINIST

Yehudi Menuhin

EDITED BY
CHRISTOPHER HOPE

HEINEMANN : LONDON

William Heinemann Ltd
10 Upper Grosvenor Street, London W1X 9PA
LONDON MELBOURNE TORONTO
JOHANNESBURG AUCKLAND

First published 1986
Copyright © Yehudi Menuhin 1986
SBN 434 46300 0

Photographs © Malcolm Crowthers 1986
Illustrations © Julian Burton 1986

Grateful acknowledgments are due to the following students
of the Yehudi Menuhin School: Lu-Szu Ching, Harvey De
Souza, Helen Hawthorne, Tasmin Little

Printed and bound in Great Britain by
Butler & Tanner Ltd, Frome and London

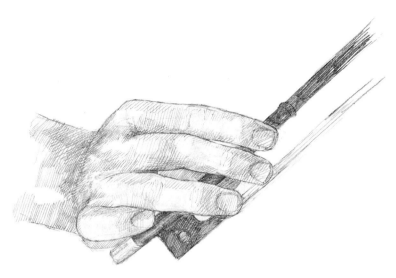

Contents

v

Prefatory note

Life Class has evolved over the years. It does not set out practices and principles which are supposed to replace or supersede the ways of other musicians, or teachers of the violin dedicated to other methods.

Certain artistic decisions, experiences, encounters in the life of a musician serve to exercise the mind and strengthen the musical character just as certain exercises keep the body supple and adaptable. I wish to set down some of these experiences and exercises as they have crucially affected the only violinist I feel I can comment on with any authority – myself.

This is not a book about what I have learnt, but about what I am learning and relearning each day.

There are three stages of learning:

- By example and imitation.
- By being formally taught. In this process the pupil's analytical and critical faculties are awakened, the range of emotional language and expression grows ever richer and the wider dimensions of style become apparent.
- By teaching oneself, taking advantage of every hint, example, opportunity, encounter with colleagues, master and private study.

All three stages are at all periods concurrent.

YEHUDI MENUHIN
April 1986

An introduction

This book contains two different strands: a discussion of my chosen way of life as a musician and violinist and, arising out of that, some of the exercises which I have evolved consistently for over half a century to help me in this way of life. The reflections, exercises, meditations, hints, guesses, prejudices and testimonies which comprise the book are offered as a whole, to be taken together. They are not commandments on how to practise or what to play. Rather, they are one musician's approaches to and preparations for his profession.

The exercises in this book have been evolved by me over many decades and it goes without saying that I have all my life tried to keep my body in a state of mobility and physical fitness. I must therefore caution everyone who attempts the more rigorous yoga-based exercises for the first time that they should be approached gently and on no account should they be forced.

ABOUT PLAYING THE VIOLIN

My main principle in playing is all-embracing and straightforward: a striving for equilibrium. Perfect equilibrium is, of course, an unattainable ideal, a complex and infinitely multifaceted thing. None the less one can approach something like the right equilibrium when one realises that no part of the body moves without some corresponding reaction or compensation in some other part, in the same sense that not a leaf falls without altering the equilibrium of the earth. A sense of subtle shifts and balances is our goal. Subtlety knows no limit.

It isn't simply a question of understanding the workings of bodily movement; that is a question of mechanics. The principle that I wish to put forward is that each part of the body moves best when it moves in harmony with other bones, muscles, limbs. To me violin playing is that procedure by which the body of the player becomes aware of itself and of its internal harmony. The principle is grasped not intellectually but through sensation, through becoming aware of the subtle checks and balances which, when properly understood, permit ease of technique.

Once the student learns to feel his or her way around the violin then the way is open to move to ever more subtle planes. The progression resulting from the many parts of the body demanding recognition, that is to say inclusion, in the free flow of movement will become clear. For what is not included becomes an obstacle, a blockage to the free flow of movement which can only impede the musician. This progress to ever subtler sensation in performance is fed by a corresponding development of sensitivity in emotional response. The fruit of this is a better balance and communication between the musician and his instrument, the musician and his audience, the musician and his music.

The instinct for continuous refinement I find very fascinating and I detect it in all civilisations. That is not to say it is always achieved, but it is an instinct in developing human consciousness to observe and register in a more concentrated fashion smaller and smaller details. This is true of cooking, of bathing, of massage, of making love, of writing poetry, and of playing the violin.

However, whenever greater refinement and sensibility become the province of the select few, or are pursued to a point where they do not include the wider population, then the effect within the civilisation – and I would contend in the making of music, and certainly in the composing of music – becomes too effete, too precious. When this happens, those left out of the pursuit of refinement take their revenge. In music I think it likely that many forms of attenuated composition were swept away at moments of violent historical change. I think, for instance, that the French Revolution saw the sweeping away of many courtly dances and other delicate airs and graces which were seen to belong to the select few. It is when subtlety, refinement and courtesy, all admirable in themselves, become codified, rigid and excessively

3

formalised, that people see them as redundant. The refinement, to which I believe we all aspire, is genuine only so long as it contains a leavening of spontaneity and a sense of common humanity. Music which exhibits this remains in touch with the emotions and desires of more, rather than fewer, people. On the other hand, art which turns its back on the often bleak life which very many people endure simply cannot last.

I sometimes think that there is something faintly Einsteinian about the discoveries the violinist makes. The violinist discovers that nothing is ever absolutely at rest, but all is in motion. Then, too, there is the discovery that space, speed and time are not unconnected but relative to one another and influenced by one another. The speed at which you play determines the space available. The more notes you play within a given time, that is to say the faster you play, so the space you occupy decreases. There is the further discovery that space is not straight but curved. The violinist, in his stance, in the way he holds the instrument, in the way he moves, recognises this curvature. This underlying organic unity is not an intellectual theory but a fact of nature. All matter, I believe, is shaped by it and I believe further that it is through our recognition of this organic unity that we make the discoveries about ourselves and our universe which carry us forward. If one looks at the pyramids one finds incredibly precise and astronomically aligned monuments, but they are monolithic constructions. Later we have columns, which begin to reflect a sense of space. There follow the dome, the arch, the cantilever – man's constructions reflecting the progressive discovery of the possibilities of space and flow. Man might have discovered and imitated all of these shapes earlier: he certainly would have observed them in nature – in rocks that had been gouged out by rivers, in natural bridges and chasms. But the uncovering of space had to take place in time. It was the same with the evolution of movement. Early man must have seen rocks roll down a hill, but to put an axle between two wheels and have a load bearing on the axle . . . there was a leap forward! It was the same with flight. Observation or, if you like, prejudice, told us that everything heavier than air would fall. But as soon as we added speed to a fixed wing we disproved the old prejudice. Speed became an integral part of shape and motion. What was regarded as fixed and constant seemed to flow. Once we had speed, we had to discover methods by which time could be more accurately measured. Movement, space, time, shape and motion became integrated into a vision of things that now seems familiar and logical. This process of discovery suggests to me that human history is characterised by a certain tenacious blindness consisting of prejudice, superstition and lethargy very reluctantly giving way to light, to clarity and to what finally appears as the obvious.

The musician's life is also a search for enlightenment and harmony. The reflections which follow are the personal testament of that perishable commodity, the working violinist.

WHY EXERCISE?

When one is playing the violin the mind should be continuously engaged in routine checking. This should become a kind of mental second nature. You should be

5

monitoring every part, every movement, checking on whether the shoulder is floating easily, the neck free, the finger, the elbow, the wrist, the feet, all easy, relaxed, coordinated. Then the breathing, the position of the eyes, the swing of the body: are they all in step, all in harmony? There should be nothing arbitrary about the movements of the violinist, nothing moving without total support from all other parts.

Continuous experiments can be made. Increasing numbers of new exercises can be invented to help one towards this end. Doubtless there are many I have forgotten and many hundreds more that I shall rediscover or invent myself. But the aim behind them remains the same: improved awareness. Once the violinist is launched on this road and is awakened to the improvements in sensation he will find this leads to greater joy, greater elation, greater abandonment, greater freedom – to lightness, subtlety, opportunity, and he will arrive at that stage where his own imagination, his own ideas, leave an imprint on every note he plays. As soon as he discovers that he is on the right way, and whether that discovery takes a week or a month or thirty years to reach, he will never fail to improve. The effects will be felt in the musician, I am convinced, and also in the music, for the music will become a carrier of the musician's own inner harmony. As he or she improves, so the music's compelling, convincing, persuasive powers will increase in the same proportion.

WHY THE VIOLIN?

It seems to me that there is a particular and distinguish-

6

able attraction about the violin which differs crucially from that of other instruments. A child who has a direct natural inclination for the violin has something of an advantage in choosing this instrument over others. The configuration of elements that guide the very young musician to the violin must be somewhat different to the ones that might lead the child, say, to the piano. For one thing, a fiddle is a much more tactile instrument. The child is immediately at home with the feel, the shape, the touch, the sound of it. Then, too, it is rather like the voice. One could suggest that the violin is the voice objectified. That is to say it is the voice heard through the medium of another instrument. And, last but not least, the violin comes in a variety of sizes. It can be made to measure.

The piano, by contrast, is a larger and more intellectual proposition. It encompasses a far greater range in pitch, volume and polyphonic capacity. The keyboard is already there, which means that when you begin to study it you are beginning at another, more adult, level. The piano is not small, it is certainly not manageable, it is not something one puts one's arms around. Quite the contrary; indeed the piano presents a bright set of teeth upon a heavy, mechanical body. The keyboard itself does not alter or vary with one's age. You cannot begin small with the piano as you do with the violin and change instruments as your age and size increase. To get the most from the piano you need to grasp a kind of intellectual grid which involves harmonic progression. Although the piano can convey a melodic effect if played by a great artist, it is not itself a melodic instrument.

Of course there are those musicians, and I have

7

known many of them with Kreisler and Enesco coming immediately to mind, who play both violin and piano. There is no doubt that the piano is a most useful instrument, particularly when one is looking at a score and it is perfectly possible to marry the two together. Eventually the player will find it more or less possible to do the same things on both instruments. So it is not that I am arguing that there is something exclusive about the violin, none the less the approach to the instrument is markedly different.

I return to the natural affinities of the child for the violin. One can see clearly the reasons for it. The violin relates exceptionally well to its user and the child can pick up the violin as easily as he picks up his teddy bear. With the violin you have to make your own sound and pitch. In fact, it is your own voice that you are projecting, or, in the case of a child, learning to project. The piano comes with its voice ready-made. Although you can distinguish a great pianist's touch, this is a sophisticated distinction. Whereas the sound, tone and style of different violinists are immediately distinguishable, the reason being that playing the violin involves the whole body much more so than the piano does. The piano involves all the extremities, the feet, the fingers and the head. The violin involves everything that goes in between, neck, arms, elbows, legs. Somehow the violin lends itself to an early twinning with its master – or perhaps I should say with its victim!

The violin is a melodic instrument. If a child sings or has heard friends or parents singing, and if he or she has much to express emotionally, then these are the things that lead to the violin. A child's voice is a high

8

voice and so the violin is perhaps more naturally approached than the cello which has a deeper voice. And then again, the cello is rather large, it is not as mobile, you cannot walk around the room playing a cello. Of course, the child with a natural bent for mathematics, for order, for the theory of music, may very well be attracted to the piano because it is, in musical terms, a much more literal instrument. The violinist if he has a beautiful tone can get away with murder, rather like the tenor can. It is perfectly possible to have an idiot tenor – if the tenor has a glorious voice. If a tenor is also intelligent, then it is a gift of the heavens. Generally it is enough if he can sing, if he can move us, if the sob is in the voice. And to some extent you can hear this with the great violinists of past days. They did not need to bother too much about style or chamber music, or even how others played. They did not have to hear other voices. They only had to hear their own.

The pianist has to listen a little more objectively, has to grasp form, and musical composition for the piano is full of many more notes than music for the violin, not only because of polyphonic capacities but also because the note clusters and arpeggios must be arranged in different sequences. The pianist must employ all the fingers and can play notes much more quickly than the violinist. The violinist has only four fingers and he can achieve nothing like the speed of the pianist's passage work or the tone clusters or the tremendous virility and seeming power. But these are all very difficult things for the child. And they also require a different mental configuration.

When I heard violin recitals by Kreisler, Heifetz and Elman, I rejoiced that they played in such totally different ways. But then every violinist plays in a different way even if he comes from the same school. I think the most homogeneous orchestra I ever encountered was in Lubliana in Yugoslavia, where for a time Ševčik, or one of his pupils, lived and the whole orchestra went through the drill. Even the Russian method with Auer, who taught Heifetz, Zimbalist and Elman, has not produced exactly matching violinists. How could it do so? Each one has his own body to deal with, long or short limbs, weight, manner of producing the sound.

Of course when we teach the child with talent, we recognise that gift. We also know that we are building on basic strength. It is that basic strength, developed in childhood, which will carry the violinist through life and, one hopes, will help that violinist to avoid the many pitfalls that lie ahead. The child dreams of playing the violin, of going straight to the end result without any of the painful intervening stages. Actually such blithe innocence is very good in one sense because it carries him through those difficult stages. The flexibility of the growing child allows it to absorb quite a lot of distortion because the child will grow out of distortion. That potential reaches its term when the body is no longer growing, when it can no longer absorb these abuses or wrong handling. At that point the violinist has to begin working rationally, searching out his own way and becoming accountable for the way he makes music. It is at this stage that the early training, if it has been properly organised, should begin to pay off.

On the other hand, the child who has been put to work beneath the draconian eye of the parent or the ambitious teacher and has been made to practise for six or eight hours a day may experience great difficulties later, as has been the case of quite a few violinists who afterwards broke down, sometimes committed suicide, or went off their heads. I am sad to say I have known cases like that.

If you have, as it were, become entirely dependent on untroubled hours of practice administered with Prussian discipline, then, of course, when you have to find your way in the world, to find time for all the things a human being must do, then naturally the tensions begin to build. Often you cannot afford the hours of practice you once undertook at the expense of living. In his narrow and rigorous upbringing, our young violinist has had time for nothing else, time for no chamber music, time for really no music of any sort except the narrow regime of his fiddle. And then he finds himself in the position where, not having spread his interests sufficiently widely and no longer being able to work as he once did, as if he had all the time in the world and absolutely nothing else to do but play the violin, he is slowly torn apart by competing interests, contending calls on his time. Public life, married life, children, duties, obligations, every hour, every minute must be weighed against the steadily diminishing prospect of fewer and fewer years in which to practise and perfect one's art. For, as all violinists know, there must come a time when one simply cannot continue any longer.

Now to live under this lowering sky is a very exhausting and extremely taxing existence. That is why the first fine rapture of the young violinist, which carries him through any number of difficulties, is to be valued and nurtured in the early years and care taken to develop as fully as possible all aspects of life and musical style. It is at this young age that the natural links between the child and an instrument such as the violin are most readily appreciated and built upon.

There is a further appeal which I believe the violin holds for the imaginative child. Certainly from my youngest years I believed the violinist to be a romantic, itinerant figure. Perhaps this had to do with the fact that all the violinists I heard were born elsewhere, somewhere far away from San Francisco. It was with a flood of recognition that I found this to be true when I encountered the gypsies in Romania when I was eleven. Something instinctive inside me responded to the way in which their music expressed my own longings and despairs and sadnesses. This recognition worked in me as it must have worked in thousands of Russian Jewish violinists and is now working in the same way on many people of many cultures, this longing for emancipation, for a voice which liberates.

The violin is the poor man's instrument but it is, strangely enough, also the instrument which offers to the individual the greatest and most immediate means of expression. It enables a person, a people, to speak for and of themselves. I recall visiting a museum for folk instruments in Moscow and I could not believe my eyes when I saw hundreds upon hundreds of varieties of violins, every conceivable shape, size, design, form – some of them didn't even look like violins. Yet all were played on four strings with a bow and were made by the village carpenter or village handyman and could be carried about the place. These hard-working, hard-wearing fiddles were rustic folk instruments of infinite resource. Such an instrument was sturdy. If it got wet or damaged it could be easily repaired or replaced.

The instrument for country folk, for Jews and gypsies – that heritage lies at the heart of the violinist's calling. I believe Jews and the gypsies exchanged or learnt a great deal from one another, particularly in the southern part of Russia and in Romania. The melodies of the gypsies are not dissimilar to the Hasidic melodies my father sang. I remember he was struck by that and so, of course, was Enesco. This instrument that existed at every level: in the poorest village where it was played at weddings and dances as Marc Chagall has reminded us in his paintings. A poor man's instrument, there was never any question of it being more than that, but one which culminates in the fine instruments of Stradivari and the Italian violin makers, which are a world, a universe away from the fiddle's rough beginnings – summations of what I might call aural carpentry!

When you think about it, this rough-and-ready approach to the instrument is genuine, authentic and probably almost forgotten in the best schools of violin playing. Rough and ready, and yet the violin is a frail instrument: its strings break, it has to be tuned continually, and the bow must be adjusted. So the fiddler learns to make do. He must learn to get along with his instrument. I sometimes think that this is what is missing from the modern violin school and its methods. They do not teach the student to pick up the violin and do something with it. Do anything – and everything – with it. This is why I look to the child who, with the child's confidence, is willing to take up the fiddle, to play it and to play *with* it, to explore its infinite range of tones and qualities until he finds that voice which is uniquely his own.

Exercises: 1

LIVING ON YOUR FEET

The violinist's future rests, as it were, on the feet. One needs to learn to open the toes and to strengthen the arches. Remember that the violinist seldom takes the weight off his feet. Fallen arches, bad displacement of weight and stiffness in the feet deprive you of necessary elasticity; they are also painful and unhelpful.

I believe that the violinist should be built from the ground up. In carrying out these exercises, all of which are done on the floor and range from exercises for spreading the toes to simple breathing exercises, it is possible that you will confirm an observation I have made. This is that a natural reaction occurs in the hand when one is exercising the foot. Even without intending to do so you may notice that the hand wants to do the same thing as the foot.

TOES

I suggest sitting down for this so as to have a close and clear view of the feet. Rest as much weight as possible on the exercising foot, which should be placed solidly on the floor (1).

14

FIGURE I

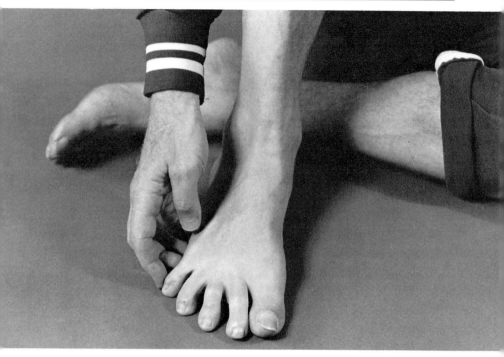

FIGURE 2

Now spread the toes as widely apart as possible, letting your finger rest lightly on the small toe (2). Push the toes together while attempting to resist the pressure of the finger with the toes.

Do this with each foot in turn.

ARCHES

Still seated as for the previous exercise, let the exercising foot lie flat on the floor and at rest. Then brace the foot, stretching the toes up and outwards so they are splayed.

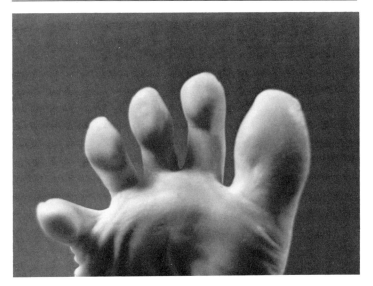

FIGURE 3

You will notice that the arch deepens. Hold the braced position for a steady count of ten, then relax.

Repeat three times with each foot.

Remember that you have an outer as well as an inner arch. If correctly done, the exercise raises and strengthens the outer arch as well.

AND TOES AGAIN

Sit or lie on the floor for this exercise. Make sure the feet and toes are relaxed, then stretch the toes on both feet out as much as possible (3). Hold for a steady count of ten.

Sit on the floor with your legs stretched out before you. Curve the toes downwards, hold for the count of five, then relax.

17

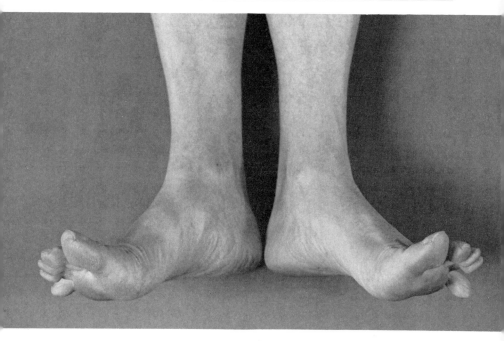

FIGURE 4

Then stretch the toes upwards, towards your body (4). Notice how the feet take on the same position as in the exercise for the arches. Hold for the count of five, then relax. Alternate between downward and upward toe stretches.

STRETCHING

This is an exercise which stretches several parts of the body: toes, feet, ankles, legs, groin, sides, shoulders and neck. Sit with one leg tucked in as much as possible (5) and stretch the other leg out along the floor, keeping it

FIGURE 5

straight. Grasp the big toe, turn your body sideways and try to look over the shoulder furthest from the out-stretched leg. Twist the body round as much as you can, feeling the stretch along the back of your leg and in your sides and groin. (Hold for the count of ten.) Repeat the process with the other leg. (Do this six times on each side.)

Next stretch both legs straight out in front, and, keeping them slightly apart, bend forward and grasp the big toes or the complete sets of toes. (If at first you cannot reach your toes, start by gripping your ankles, or as low down your legs as possible.) Then, keeping the backs of

FIGURE 6

the legs pressed down against the floor and the lower back pressed forward as much as possible, pull on the toes. That's the secret, bend and pull.

THE GALLOP

I call this the gallop because the rhythm is rather like that of a horse at the run. It is an exercise of opposites, of counterweights. As the right leg comes up, moving to the left, so the arms begin to move to the right.

Kick the right leg up and over to the left; this will roll the body onto its left side. Move the arms in the opposite direction to balance the body's weight.

When the body is on its left side and the full extent of the stretch has been reached (6), repeat the movements using the left leg. Try to build up a rhythm. Count a time to yourself. Six gallops in each direction is enough.

BREATHING

Breathing exercises are ideal for relaxation. I enjoy doing this one in the lotus position (7), but it is not necessary. Sit in a comfortable position, upright and balanced. Hold the nose just below the bridge between thumb and fore-finger. Block the right nostril and breathe in through the left to a slow steady count of five. Now block the left and breathe out through the right to the same steady count. Set up a rhythm: breathe in through the left, block the left; breathe out through the right, block the right. You can vary the count to suit yourself, aiming at slow steadiness but not forcing yourself into uncomfort-able slowness.

The basic principle

There is a basic principle in using the breath which I have found comes quite naturally after a little practice. It should form the basis of all exercising. Those irritating commands you remember from childhood – injunctions to 'sit up straight', or 'pull your stomach in' – are quite empty of meaning unless you understand the use to which you put the breath you draw into your body. The correct instruction should be, *Breathe against the resistance of your spine.* That is to say, imagine the breath you take as a balloon filling your lungs, stomach, abdomen and pushing against your spine.

The feeling I am trying to convey can be experienced in the following way:

- Lie down on the floor.
- Keep the small of the back pressed firmly against the floor.
- Breathe in deeply against the resistance of the floor pressing against the flat back.
- Breathe out against the same resistance.
- Now stand up and breathe deeply, feeling the balloon of air pressing against your spine.

This exercise can be cultivated when lying, standing, walking and playing the violin.

A little practice and concentration will pay dividends. You will find your body more alive, aware of itself, feeling lighter and more resistant to fatigue.

Breathing exercises can also be done in bed before getting up in the morning. So can many others – with

23

minimal disturbance to a sleeping partner! It is surprising how many movements can be made with the head and with parts of the face and head. For instance, we can move the skin on our scalp and feel it move with our fingers; we can roll the eyes in circles and move them from side to side. We can open them wide and close them tight. Some people can move their ears. We can also massage them, following the spiral all the way from the middle to the ear lobe, massaging that area where a surprising number of nerve ends are located and where acupuncture and pressure are particularly effective. The mouth can be opened wide and then closed tightly. The tongue can press against the palate and against the teeth which are clenched. The tongue can be stuck out as far as possible and then pulled back. The chin can be moved from side to side and forward and back. The cheeks can be exercised by moving between a smile and a pout. The neck can be alternately stretched and relaxed.

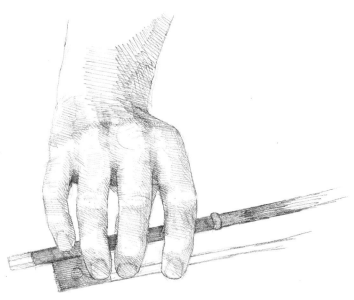

On tour

I have been touring for over fifty years and one of my more regular migratory patterns is the annual tour of the United States. For some decades I have undertaken this early in the year. It lasts for perhaps eight weeks, during which time I make twenty-five appearances in some fifteen towns and cities.

A DAY AT RANDOM

Here I am today, for instance, in Cleveland, contemplating the luxury of a whole week in one place. It is a relaxing contrast to the one-night stands, which are

25

necessary but taxing. One tends to stay longer when playing with an orchestra as there are usually two or three concerts in the same city. This means, of course, extra rehearsals, which gives a feeling of spaciousness to the visit – very welcome on a long tour. However, whether one-night stand or a more extended visit, one thing is common to both: the work. On tour it is rare, if not impossible, to stop working. One is totally encapsulated in a job which continues to make its pressures and demands felt throughout the length of the tour.

The repertoire has of course been prepared in advance. I know that in the course of the tour I shall be playing concertos by Berg, Elgar, Bruch and Beethoven. There are also various pieces for my different recitals. I shall be including something I haven't done in years – Handel's E minor sonata – and also some delightful small pieces by Debussy, Kreisler and Bloch. My performance of these works must be polished, it must be refined, it must be kept fresh. To allow myself a chance of achieving this I choose to refuse all social engagements wherever possible. I've kept to that here in Cleveland, with the exception of a small party after the first concert. My only other concession has been to an old friend whom I've known ever since I was a boy here in Cleveland. It is well over fifty-five years ago now when we first met and played with electric trains together. He's an old and charming friend, now confined to a wheelchair, and I enjoy lunching with him and his wife. For the rest, my contacts during the day tend to be telephonic, and usually no more than two or three. First of all, of course, there is my wife Diana. There may be loose ends to tie up with management in New York or with the office in

London; there may be an appointment to be made with a friend, or a telephone interview. But where time and concentration both find their fullest, purest focus and purpose is in the music and in playing the violin.

The experience of working quietly, of belonging to the violin, of that instrument's having, for the period of the tour, supremacy over every other consideration, is in many ways deeply satisfying. Perhaps the existence I have described, this picture of me incarcerated in my hotel cell sounds unduly restricted, but the truth is quite the contrary – there is great freedom in this isolation. There is, for a start, simply the practical aspect of it: I don't have to struggle to find the time to practise and reflect, as I might have to do at home or in normal circumstances. Here the violin is with me day and night, a constant companion, seldom silent. It can sound very sweetly and, when properly approached, makes abundant compensation for the hours one puts into it. The day bears no resemblance to an office day. One is freed, to a great extent, from the tyranny of time; the hours are not necessarily fixed, except for rehearsals with orchestra and possibly with one's pianist. Even the latter can be shifted. So the day is really determined by one's own inclinations. There is something special about the isolation of this life with its sudden bursts of public performance: the wonderful satisfaction of having worked towards the best performance I can give, of receiving the appreciation of my colleagues, of having given a period of sustained concentration, a genuine slice of my life, to the main concern – which is also my vital interest.

So then, how do I go about it? It's not time on my hands, but *in* my hands. I may get up, and after various

27

rituals – including a hot shower, my exercises and then perhaps rest – I may feel like sitting down and looking at the music. I may not feel like plunging immediately into practising. The practice will come, but in its good time. The important thing is to approach the practice session without pressure, with the feeling that the day is there for it to be done. It is important, too, to be in a suitable state of mind and heart, relaxed in body and spirit, ready to begin. Happily, the violin asks to be handled. Aesthetically, the violin is the most glorious object and one of my housekeeping pleasures is to polish it every few weeks and put on a new set of strings. To the ear it is a delight, especially if, as I do, one practises with a mute; the sound then is low and sweet and soft. I use the big, heavy metal mute which I find very relaxing as it allows me to concentrate on most aspects of the performance without having to listen continually to the full sound. I do that listening on the stage; after many years of experience it comes as a matter of course. The main thing for me is to know how to make the sounds, not the concert sound, and to make them to and for myself in every way correctly, lacking only the final dimension of projection. I think it is very important to preserve the projection, not to exhaust oneself with what would amount to constant public performances in private. Practice is an affair between the musician and his instrument, it is not intended for the ears or the eyes of outsiders.

Playing the violin is, of course, also a matter of touch. It is sensual; the fingers are as much affected as the ears. The violin is an extremely delicate object of touch; its vibrating strings live, and the action of the fingers on them has to be extremely accurate, sensitive and balanced.

If the outside world does not often break in on me as I work in my hotel room, I occasionally communicate with it. On impulse I may ring one of my children, or a friend. The telephone is my lifeline. Some people are impulse buyers, I suppose I must be an impulse caller. From my telephone conversations I receive a certain intellectual, abstract friendship, a kind of long-distance companionship. The violin by contrast provides the immediate companionship of a living presence. The roles that normally apply in the world seem to be inverted while on tour. Human beings seem remote, approachable only in conversation, while the violin is there, approachable in the senses.

It's quite amazing what periods of incarceration in a hotel bedroom can allow one to achieve. Several times when I have had to work to prepare a new work or a new programme I have done it by this method of total immersion. I can remember resurrecting the Shostakovich concerto for a concert in Zurich. I had three days in an hotel in Vienna to prepare it and I worked around the clock. It didn't really matter whether it was day or night. I slept when I felt the need. As soon as I was awake and well disposed I practised for as long as I felt I could continue. When tired I went to sleep, without any regard for what was going on around me. This may seem to be a rather ascetic existence but in fact I find it emotionally and intellectually satisfying. It is not lonely. On the contrary such periods of seeming isolation are full of beautiful music and the inexpressible satisfaction of searching for, and testing yourself against, an ideal of perfection. In this method of working there lies the daily discovery of new refinements, new possibilities, endless rewards of leisure. With regard to playing the violin. I continually discover that there are areas of great fascination and importance as yet unexplored.

And of course one must eat. There is something to be said, however, for eating alone because while you miss the joy of company, solo meals never interfere with work. There is no incentive to dawdle over the two or three meals with which the day is punctuated.

I always get in a supply of the sort of food that I like. In this way not only do I get what I want to eat but I maintain insofar as possible my self-sufficiency. I get in the basics: bran, wheat germ, plenty of fruit, and yoghurt wherever possible. This is no problem in large cities, where health food shops are multiplying all the time and where good bread is also obtainable. I like bread made with wheat, rye and barley, breads that have raisins and nuts and bean sprouts. One gets to know the cities for what they can offer by way of food; New York, for instance, is always good for dairy products, goats' milk, yoghurt and cheese, for fresh vegetables and salads. There is room service of course, which provides a menu. From time to time I'm tempted, I order fish, salad, potato or some sort of vegetable; perhaps a soup. But never, never, do I touch alcohol, sugar, white bread or desserts. These days one also has to be wary of shellfish. Every few weeks I might order a broiled lobster, but even my beloved American clams I have learnt to treat with suspicion, and must look askance these days at oysters and shrimps. Of course I am very careful to avoid all the little titbits that you tend to find in your room; those

wedges of wrapped cheeses into which almost everything goes except perhaps cheese, that bottle of wine,
those prepared and packaged foods full of chemicals and
cancer-producing substances. In fact, travelling in
America has left me increasingly convinced that it is a
suicidal society. The saccharine which comes in little
pink packets carries the inscription, 'This product may
be hazardous to your health for saccharine is proven to
have caused cancer in laboratory animals.' It must be
said, though, that it is odd how people seem to thrive
on these very dubious concoctions. Or at least the in-
dustry supplying them thrives. What I sometimes won-
der is whether this attitude really is terminal – or is it
perhaps the horribly carefree final fling of a last generation?

Contained, not to say cooped and confined (though
with no feeling of confinement), in my hotel room another requirement is exercise. Travelling by plane the
other day I happened to see in a magazine an advertise-
ment for a very typically American assortment of original gifts to help the athletically minded. Here was
every kind of device; gadgets for entertaining while exercising; devices for impressing your friends; and an interesting gadget offering the pleasures of cross-country
skiing without ever leaving the comfort of your bedroom. You simply slip your feet into the holders designed
to take them and swing along happily without getting
anywhere. The advertisers claimed it to be absolutely
excellent for hips and stomach muscles. I found it interesting to try the exercise without the machine. Ameri-
cans have a great love for putting a machine between
them and the object which they seek to attain. In the

case of cross-carpet skiing, as I call it, it is quite possible and rather fun to slide the feet backwards and forwards; and after an experiment I was able to corroborate what the advertisers said – the hips and stomach do benefit from the exercise far more than they would in ordinary walking and running because in this exercise you are having to force the foot against the resistance of the ground. After doing it for some ten minutes or so I found I could run twice as fast and lightly around my bedroom of course. I find this is often preferable to walking the streets for which, in any event, I have little time, few opportunities and almost no desire. I do not find them particularly edifying and they can be unsafe.

Even a fiddler on the hoof must settle somewhere, however briefly. For frankly I carry the tools of my trade with me. It's the nature of the work I do that leaves me free to create my own atmosphere. Someone will send flowers or fruit and I just stay put. I prefer to have a room that allows me to move, to run up and down, to spread myself about, so I generally rearrange the furniture. The coffee table is largely useless to me (I don't entertain), so I put it somewhere against the wall. Its only use for me is as a place to put my violin case and anything else that comes along, so clearing as much of the centre of the room as possible for exercises, for running and for practice space. In this bedroom, today in Cleveland, my window looks out over Lake Erie where everything is icy. I have moved the furniture around to give me much more space in the middle of the room and a space before the window. I have also turned the bed around; it was placed east-west and I prefer sleeping north-south. I have to say that the maid was rather astonished to find the position of the furniture totally altered. But I feel more at home this way. There are times when I do not envy pianists; their life is not an easy one. It's rare for them to have a piano in their room and they must get up and dress and go out in search of some horrible little studio to practise in. A pianist leads a much more exposed and difficult life.

Now however well organised I am for my daily music there are things which unavoidably break in upon my solitude. If I don't venture out, that is not to say that others do not venture in. I have for instance an invitation to give a class at the Conservatory. But, alas, time will not allow. Journalists call and sometimes cannot be denied. But these days I avoid accepting invitations to give radio and television interviews. I find them unnecessary, trivial and a waste of time. Television people have a way of making you arrive an hour too early. As a result you sit around doing nothing, only to waste yet more time being made up – to then sit and answer silly questions for three minutes. I don't do that if I can possibly avoid it. I am not being superior – for I do admire some of these superb, seven-days-a-week TV chatterers, who come so prepared with potential questions that they seem to know, and often *do* know, more about my life than I know myself.

So here I am, in Cleveland. And this year I realise that something has changed. Since I visit only every four or five years, I now have to contemplate the distinct possibility that I will not be coming back. Certainly not as a violinist. Perhaps never again. Such realisations concentrate the mind. Certainly they colour my communication with the audience, and that audience after all includes many people who have known me for over half a century. Thus my concert will take on a particular quality: there will be in it something that makes each communication of sound, gesture, tone, idea, a little more important and precious.

A VIOLINIST'S SHOPPING LIST

Diet

wheat germ
wheat bran
yoghurt
honey
molasses
kelp
bone meal
vitamin preparations
minerals (all prepared as naturally as possible)
whole-grain bread
fresh fruit organically grown if possible
cottage cheese
sprouted grain
salads of all kinds
soya oil, or thistle oil (which is the lightest oil available) and sesame oil
cider vinegar
vegetable salt or sea salt (vegetable salt is actually much better – both salts should be used very sparingly)
ginseng
royal jelly (excellent for the stomach)
mineral water
sour milk

various herb teas, camomile, ribena, rose hip
bath essences (excellent for circulation)

Concert essentials

molat
lecithin
a banana and an orange for vitamin C
eau-de-Cologne, or a body rub of some sort made of pine
    essence
a little alcohol (to clean the fingerboard of the violin)
very fine metal wool (to wipe the resin off strings and
    fingerboard)

Other options

I am extremely interested in Chinese medicines.
a German preparation called *Medvitan*, a useful prepar-
    ation against colds. It's taken by injection and per-
    fectly painless. If ever I sneeze I give myself an injec-
    tion of *Medvitan*.
a very fine fruit kefir called *Rifek*.
something I haven't tasted, but would love to, is koumiss
    (this is fermented mare's milk, available in Mongolia).

ACCOMPANISTS, ACCOMPLICES AND
STRATAGEMS ON TOUR

My first companions were my family and, in particular,
my father. One should not forget that the solo violinist
is generally accompanied, usually by a pianist. I always
think of it rather as some Don Quixote travelling with
Sancho Panza. Your accompanist can be many things:

35

companion; likeable scoundrel; he can be a real musician; a great support and sympathetic character – or he can make touring a most weary business indeed!

I have had very good companions: I think of Marcel Gazelle; Adolph Baller was superb; and, in my young days, Artur Balsam, a very wonderful musician. We were good pals. We did not spend too many nights on the town, mind you, but we had a great sense of adventure in choosing schedules. We could always find a quicker and more direct connection than the plan allowed for. You grow very attached inevitably to your accompanist. You eat, work, practise together and inevitably a firm bond springs up. Perhaps the only pianist I have played with regularly, though she was not strictly speaking only an accompanist, was my sister, Hephzibah. More recently, I have played with Paul Coker, a charming companion, good natured and self-reliant. I do not like to waste more time rehearsing than is absolutely necessary. In the old days I rehearsed endlessly with an accompanist. My present accompanists come ninety per cent prepared. I am sometimes accompanied by my son, Jeremy, with whom it is great fun to be on tour because we really share so much. I hope I may modestly claim to have given my son a particular way of analysing music. As a result it is an enormous pleasure when we go through the music together and is a huge bond between us.

So, whether I travel alone or whether I travel with an accompanist or, as so often happens, with accompanist and my wife Diana making a kind of trio, there are advantages in the support of the right companions. Life on the road is demanding and many challenges test the stamina, musicianship, not to say the patience, of the fiddler on the hoof.

If the itinerant musician, who must play for his supper, must sometimes resist the hostility of the world, perhaps its applause is more dangerous. One has to be on one's guard against over-appreciation, against the love and fellow feeling, not to say the tribute, that sometimes follow a fine performance. I think I can testify in all modesty to the remarkable effect that a beautiful performance can have on people who come to meet the artist backstage. The reason for this is an interpretation of the work and a standard of performance which have moved the audience and satisfied the artist. To achieve this result they have about them an extra quality of penetration, understanding, tenderness and gratitude, which seems immediately to give a radiance to almost any contact that follows the experience. It is as if a good interpretation of a work in a public place acts on the audience to create a mode of understanding, and of mutual warmth, which then colours the contacts that follow. In this way one meets and makes many friends.

However, there is a danger in taking for granted this positive reaction of gratitude and of dividing the rest of the world into those who bring tribute and those who do not. It is a danger which commonly attends those in power who, if they allow it to continue, are eventually surrounded only by flatterers. Human nature being what it is, it becomes all too easy to expect praise and then to be childishly disappointed if someone coming backstage does not comment on the 'superlative' performance – let alone if they have something critical to say.

The extreme reactions, not to say the adulation,

which certain musicians evoke, and the violinist is certainly among these (he has been from Paganini onwards, an enormously romantic figure), is perhaps due to the fact that a musician's life is acutely susceptible to the expression, indeed the generation, of emotions. They are integral to his art. The emotions which music arouses grow out of something the Germans call *Übermut*, that profuse, extravagant abandon, which we associate with spring, with love, and with passion. Music is a measure of the powers that inhabit us, be they beatific or demonic, and which we try to keep in balance and to which sometimes we yield. This last is the best reason why those musicians who perhaps suffer from an excess of adulation are wise to be on their guard. After all, the very last thing a musician could feel himself to be is self-righteous. A musician is by nature someone who has lived and sinned, someone who remembers his feelings, his weaknesses, so that the contrition he feels and the touch of nostalgia and remorse become part of the very music he is playing and that is why it will move an audience whose frailties the musician shares.

Exercises: 2

BENDING AND STRETCHING

Touching your toes is an old standby, useful just the same – as long as you always keep your knees straight! There are interesting variations in hand positioning, which are beneficial.

38

FIGURE 8 ▶

You can touch the floor with the fingers extended forward (8), or place the palms flat on the floor, fingers together and pointing forward. You can let the arms and hands hang limply so that the backs of the fingers brush the floor, or you can stretch your arms out forwards and touch the floor as far in front of you as possible with your fingertips.

RELAXING THE NECK

This is also a well-known exercise for violinists, and none the worse for that. It is a paramount requirement of violin playing that the neck should be free, without any constriction.

Let the neck relax and the head fall forward. The sensation should be of the head falling – you are not forcing the head, but moving the body in such a way that the head cannot help moving if the neck is relaxed. Now bend to one side (9), then forwards, to the other side, and back, letting the head roll round in a complete circle. Repeat in the opposite direction.

Always move slowly and in a relaxed way. Three times in each direction will do.

LEARNING TO WALK

It is crucial for a violinist to know how to stand correctly – well balanced, with the head correctly held. Yet these apparently simple things are often little understood. Harmony and balance are a matter of the parts of the body working interdependently, and the following exercises help you to realise this interdependence.

40

FIGURE 9 ▶

Start by standing with the legs comfortably apart, balancing the body and taking its weight equally. Now transfer all the weight slowly onto the left leg, now onto the right.

Now experiment with moving the head and see how this affects your whole position. The head is a considerable weight. Lean the body slightly backwards – shoulders back and relaxed (10). Feel the head pulling you back. Now lean slightly forward, putting the weight on the left foot. Hold the head up straight, chin in. Begin to sense the centre line of the body and head. This is important – to be able to feel when you are balanced on the centre. Working from a centrally balanced position one is ready to move in any direction but the basic position of the body – and of the bow and violin – is a centred one.

THE PRESS UP AND
VARIATIONS

Lie face down on the floor, legs together and straight, toes pointing backwards and hands flat on the floor under the shoulders, fingers together and pointing forwards. Straighten the arms, raising the shoulders, chest and hips off the floor. Look straight ahead. Do not hunch the shoulders up round your ears.

Now jump the feet into the conventional press up position, toes flexed under and heels up towards the ceiling, legs straight and off the ground.

For variety, and a good stretch of the shoulders, push your bottom up and lower your head until it is resting on the floor (11). This may take a bit of practice. Hold

42

FIGURE 10 ▶

FIGURE II

for a steady count of five, then return to your second press up position and to your first. Relax.

There are several hand positions which can be used in conjunction with press ups, to strengthen wrists and fingers. Obviously these must be undertaken with care and gentleness, especially the first.

The hands are placed on the floor palms up, fingers pointing backwards, towards the feet (12). This is good for wrists and fingers.

The fingers can be bent, crab-like, and braced against the floor (13). Or with the hand in the normal position spread the fingers as widely as possible (14). This is a particularly useful exercise for violinists.

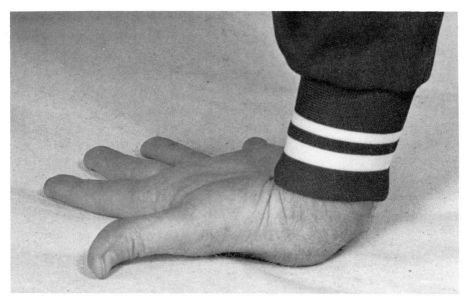

FIGURE 12

FIGURE 13

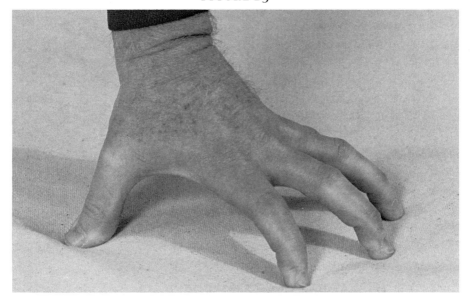

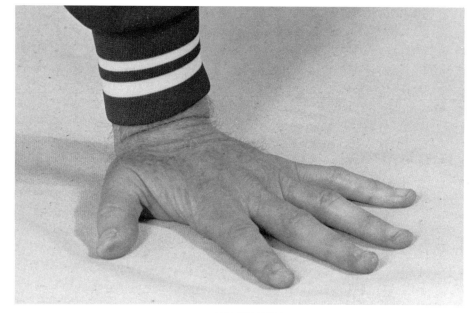

FIGURE 14

FEET UP

There is great benefit to be derived from the exercises in which the body is turned upside down: the heart is relieved of its usual workload because the blood which normally has to be pumped back up to the heart from the legs now travels towards the heart aided by gravity. Another aspect of this is that the veins and valves in the legs are no longer under strain. (It is this strain which causes varicose veins.) The brain receives refreshment from a full flow of blood.

However, these are also exercises which should be undertaken with due caution and, if you are attempting them for the first time, under qualified supervision. The shoulder stand is easier and safer to do than the head stand or plough. In shoulder stand and head stand it is advisable to enlist the aid of a friend or a wall if in any doubt as to your ability to balance, for if you fall you may twist and damage your neck. Remember, too, that in these upright positions the arms are carrying a good proportion of the body's weight – it is not being entirely taken by the head and neck.

THE SHOULDER STAND

Lie flat on your back. Bend your knees towards your face and lift your lower back onto your hands – upper arms and elbows braced against the floor. Pushing the back up with your hands, and from the shoulders, stretch the legs upwards keeping them together. By stretching the feet towards the ceiling and pressing the back you can gradually achieve a straight upright position in which the chest is pressed against your chin (15). Your neck should be straight, and solidly against the floor with your chin locked against your breastbone – but your throat relaxed. Breathe normally! Stay in the position for as long as you comfortably can, from two seconds to ten minutes – find your own level. Obviously with practice you will be able to remain up for longer periods.

It is more comfortable to do this exercise on a mat or carpet, but the surface should be firm and flat to give adequate support.

FIGURE 16

THE PLOUGH

This is an extension of the shoulder stand in which the legs are slowly and carefully lowered towards the ground beyond the top of your head. At first you may like to place a chair to receive your feet at a halfway point; with practice you will be able to place your toes on the floor. Keep the legs straight and the base of the spine stretching up towards the ceiling, and feel the way the spine is lengthened. Remember to relax muscles not being used to maintain the position, and breathe normally. (It is easy to hold the breath without even realising you are doing it when making an effort to get everything else correct!) When you feel secure in the plough position you can remove your hands from their supporting position and lie them along the floor above your head (16).

49

◀ FIGURE 15

FIGURE 17

After a few minutes in plough, take the hands back to support your back, curl the legs up and gently lower the back to the floor. Straighten up and lie flat for a few minutes, relaxing. It is important to do this after all the upside-down positions.

THE HEAD STAND

This is for those who wish to take shoulder stand and plough a stage further.

Kneel on the floor and rest the lower arms in front of you, hands linked together securely by interlacing your fingers. The hands then form a supportive brace for your head, which you place on the floor between them (17).

50

FIGURE 18

The interlaced fingers should be pressed firmly against the back of your head. Straighten your legs, so pushing your bottom into the air, and slowly walk towards your face (18). Get as near as you can. Hold this position and begin to sense how you might be able to lift your legs up into the air. Until you are ready to attempt that, finish the exercise at this point.

When you are sufficiently confident, and perhaps with the help of a friend or of a wall behind you, lift the legs up and stretch them upwards until the body is straight. Here again a friend (or a plumb-line – or both!) would be useful to tell you how straight you are. Keep the feet together. It is easier to lift the legs up in a bent position, but eventually you will be able to do it holding them straight.

Do not stay in head stand longer than you need (again 2 seconds to 10 minutes); and note that the forearms take much of the weight of the body – the hands keeping the head and neck supported.

THE HEAD STAND WITH PLUMB-LINE

This is for purists! (19)

ONE-NIGHT STANDS

This is another way of living altogether. It generally means a trip every day, though the overriding and most important consideration remains the same: to prepare for the concert that night. Everything has to be done in proper order, though of course that order will be very much more compressed. But I still find time to rest, to stretch and exercise, to warm up, to take a light meal. The pressure can sometimes be very great. One may arrive in a town with two hours to spare. If, as happens occasionally, one arrives with all afternoon ahead of one, that is a real luxury. While travelling I may be able to rest or sleep. The trick is learning how to use trains and planes to best advantage.

52

FIGURE 19 ▶

I must say that in my life I have had to warm up my fingers in some very odd places. I can remember travelling to Washington on a morning train from New York for the matinée concert. It was a five-hour trip in those days. I used to be given one of the state rooms, the private rooms at the end of the Pullman car and there I would scrape away. (At that time I had yet to discover the value of the mute.) The rest of the passengers, I recall, registered some annoyance, each coming in turn to knock furiously at the door – which was locked. I continued practising, but was uncomfortably aware that when the train arrived I should have to emerge to the malevolent glances of all those who had been suffering my music. The honourable gentlemen who occupied seats in the Pullman car were probably the kind who liked to smoke, talk or read. Certainly they did not wish to listen to a violinist practising his programme. But, since practise I must, I hit on a way to mollify these antagonistic spirits. I knew when we would be approaching Washington, as I often travelled along that route. Just as we were approaching our destination, still safely locked in my room, I played with as much expression I could muster the *Ave Maria*. The calming effect was noticeable and, the train having stopped, I was able to emerge from my room and pass the now beneficient glances of the powerful gentlemen who no longer wished to stone me.

The large state rooms in which I practised in those journeys across America and Europe were luxurious. I have experienced much more cramped conditions on rail journeys. I have often worked in a sleeper, sitting on my bunk with my knees tucked under me and plenty of pillows behind my back. Seated thus it was easy to play the G and D strings but I experienced difficulty with the E since it wasn't possible to dig the bow far enough into the mattress to allow that stroke. There was a certain pleasure in these lengthy train rides: I was able to practise, rest, sleep and read as I pleased.

THE ORCHESTRA AND ITS USES

Music is fugitive, evanescent. The orchestra works very hard to produce something which is gone almost as soon as it is achieved.

An orchestra is the very best judge of any musician. The collective opinion of the orchestra is well-nigh infallible; there is no fooling them. I proceed always on the basis of acknowledging any mistake I make immediately. Soliciting suggestions from an orchestra familiar with the work is an advisable procedure. At the same time one should not yield on a point if one is convinced of its rightness – one should at least proceed to try it. The evidence of the score, the feel of the music itself (whether it is carrying the message and the sound it should), the orchestral response, and the public response – those are the guidelines for soloist or conductor finding their bearings in interpreting a particular work.

The ebb and flow which exists between conductor and orchestra or between soloist and orchestra is something that I find remarkably satisfying. Interpreting music is a creative task but what we have in the orchestra is creativity joined with understanding, whilst the sheer physical nature of preparing the music – the effort, the humour and the fun of going about such a communal task – in no way lessens the seriousness of the effort; indeed these are all vital elements of that seriousness. There is also, when you think of it, something astonishing in giving your whole soul, your whole being to the interpretation of the works of absent composers. When I work with an orchestra I am frequently aware of the fact that I am engaged in something apparently quite irrelevant and yet miraculously more important than anything else. It is important because it is a counter, a challenge, to the grind for survival which takes place in office and factory and street, day in and day out and because there is, I believe, an unspoken assumption that the grind for survival is not the purpose and the aim of mankind, at least not the ultimate purpose. For we suspect I think, that the daily round is not the real purpose of existence, though it often purports to be. It is rather from what we create on 'stage, what we conjure out of our imagination from our ideas, ideals, dreams, in our dialogues with great creators of the past and present, that the real, the valuable and the inspiring emerge. What is there in life, after all, unless every act, every greeting, every dialogue, every cooperative effort in street and factory recognises that human life has a value and that value can be expressed in art?

But this is to approach the orchestra as conductor. There is another relationship which is more problematical; that is to approach it as soloist. As by nature and dedication the violinist is primarily a single voice expressing himself, so the discipline and the regimentation of an orchestra does not appeal to someone who has spent his first twenty years dreaming of a self-propelled career. There is the belief that the life of the soloist and that of the orchestral musician are mutually exclusive.

I can understand why that is so. I can remember a sad epoch when American and Russian orchestras were peopled by disappointed virtuosi. The strings were regimented into sections and they were never soloists as other members of the orchestra, for example the winds, really are. When I was a boy, the expressions I saw on the faces of some violinists in the back desks of the orchestra were very depressing. They trundled along and played, sometimes without much enthusiasm, and they were a burden carried by the front desks just to augment the sound. There was very little genuine participation.

I see a very different picture today. The financial position of the orchestral player in America and Europe has improved considerably. Concert-masters in the orchestras have an extensive musical knowledge and an affinity for the art which outstrips that of many soloists. The best orchestras today listen to each other, they become, in a sense, large chamber orchestras. I should mention, too, how in the absence of total individual responsibility, which the soloist carries, the communal response of the orchestra is in fact much more intuitive, instantaneous and more real, when the orchestra is working well together.

And so the aspiring violinist would do well to look at an orchestral career, and I am well aware that my words may surprise and dismay violinists aspiring to a solo career: and yet a member of the orchestra today is probably at a greater advantage. I say this as one who has seen the improvements in opportunity for orchestral members and as one who has suffered all his life the penalties of an itinerant career. I note the benefits of that other life: the regular hours, the free days, the lack of the need to tear oneself into three parts, to be able to stay in one place and cultivate musical friends, to see one's children, to be with one's husband or wife regularly, together with a regular income which compares, I can assure young violinists, very favourably with the sort of rewards the solo musician can expect. These factors will become an increasingly powerful inducement to the young musician to take up the orchestral life.

RUBATO

The art of rubato is largely lost. Rubato is the knowledge of how you mould a phrase quite freely in accordance with a succession of notes which demand that one or other, or several of them, be given more time, more sound, more expression and more especial texture, yet without disturbing the basic beat. In other words, one has been asked to do a very difficult thing, one is giving to a succession of notes a deliberate, strategic unevenness which does not in fact disturb the flow of the music. Rubato is something that jazz players ought to have, but, as they concentrate on complexities of counter-rhythms rather than flexibility of line, they often lack it, except of course for the very greatest of them. It amused me, when playing jazz with Stéphane Grappelli, to experience for the first time the services of a rhythm band, in which the players specialise in providing an absolute rhythm, while the soloist develops a free and flexible line. A classical musician is obliged to be both rhythmical and flexible. For this reason I believe that improvisation is an integral part of music making. When you improvise you do not improvise to a metronome and yet you observe a distinct pulse. There are musicians who mistake metronomic meter for pulse. Pulse is a living measure which, though fairly even, is not a military exactitude. Anyone can march to a rigid rhythm, but that is not true rhythm, that is metronome time, and keeping metronome time has nothing to do with live rhythm. In fact, people who are very strict and very superior and play music to the metronome have generally a very poor sense of rhythm. Perhaps what I mean can best be exemplified if one listens to Schubert's music. Schubert requires perhaps the most strict and the most undeviating pace of any music yet it is always richly expressive for within the rhythm there is life, there is no rigid beat but rather a sense of strolling in the woods while the mind and the heart are free to dream.

MANAGEMENTS

I am fortunate to have managers who have been my friends for many decades. Time and custom have built up a relationship of devotion and mutual trust. In fact, I can hardly call my relationship with my managers a business relationship, for while it is very correct, enveloping and protective, it is the warmth and the trusting friendship which make all the difference. I am proud to say that in the case of my French manager, Yves Dandelot is a member of the third generation of the family which has managed me. His grandfather managed my first concert in Paris in 1927. Much the same position obtains with all my other managements with the exception, of course, of the interruption in Germany in the last war. I can hardly believe that my cordial relationship with my post-war management in Germany is already over forty years old. In America I have had the same succession, if I may call it that, within my American management since 1927. It is one of the fruits and rewards of a long career that relationships with people grow and deepen over a period and, rather as with the cities one has visited often and come to hold in great affection, the relationships take on a kind of patina, a glow of warmth and pleasure whenever such acquaintances are renewed, something made up of happy memories and memorable concerts.

Never begrudge a manager his commission. If his commission seems large, remind yourself that he is working for you. You wouldn't want to waste your time selling yourself or getting engagements. Your manager does that for you. He deserves his commission.

READING

I have relatively little time to read. That being the case I do have a few books, a few dependable standbys into which I dip and have done so for many years. One of my favourites is a German translation of the sayings of Lao-tse. Of course I look at the news of the day, but that usually serves to convince me that the world is as crazy, as mad, as terrifying as it was the day before. Very few items relieve the general gloom.

A travelling musician is fulfilling this role for so much of the time that reading becomes difficult. There are certainly very few long quiet evenings in which one may curl up with a new novel or a play. Practice comes first and when practice is over generally there are other things to do, not the least of them to sleep. And so I like to have books about me that contain readable matter in small doses; a book of poems, a collection of Aesop's fables, my copy of *Gracian's Manual* – a wonderfully subversive collection of thoughts by a seventeenth-century Spanish Jesuit.

I take enormous joy from studying scores. This is particularly useful if one is stranded. So I suppose when I say that I don't have much time for reading what I should say is that my reading is largely musical. So many things fill in the time and, then, so much time is needed to concentrate, rethink, to work or to polish the music one is preparing that the hours seem all too short. Perhaps that is why I am, as far as reading matter goes, a glancer and a dipper.

AUDIENCES I HAVE KNOWN

The performing artist experiences a very palpable if intangible contact with an audience. An audience knows very well if it is about to share a performance that is assured and confident. This knowledge communicates itself immediately, and is helpful.

In my experience there are various ways of holding an audience. Some people do it aggressively – they display a certain aura of domination and even contempt. It suits some people to work in that way; it is not my way. Much depends upon the artist's perception of what an audience is. I regard my audience as good people who have gone out of their way to listen to me and come to the concert in an attitude of trust. They convey feelings of warmth and I reciprocate those feelings by my desire to play the work I have been preparing and contemplating for a long time in such a way that the audience partakes of the experience, one might almost say the *experiment*, of the work. If the experiment is successful it carries the audience along. In other words, I think the best spirit in which to approach an audience is one of cooperation and a wish to share the music.

Of course audiences vary widely. And it is not always the urban, middle-class audiences which give the best account of themselves. Take the suburban audience. Now suburbs are notoriously uncultured communities, not through any fault of their own but because great cities, and I am thinking in particular of American cities, often exist only to provide offices for daily commuters. At the end of the day the commuter goes back to his home, as a result seldom visiting theatre, opera, library or museum. So what happens these days is that culture comes out to the suburbs, where there are various halls to receive the performing musician. Not all of these venues are particularly good; sometimes they are cinemas or church halls. As one arrives one sees masses of station wagons parked outside – the insignia, the chariot of the suburban dweller, who feels somehow a little more rural driving a station wagon. Typically it is packed with children and lettuces and cabbages and shopping bags and so on. Such audiences are often very polished, by which I mean not only that the finger nails are very clean and everyone uses deodorant, but also that everyone is accustomed to getting their music on the radio or sometimes on television, just by twiddling knobs. And as I play at these concerts sometimes I have the unmistakable feeling that my audience would love to be twiddling the knob to see what is on the other station, to see what is on the programme which is being watched next door, just to compare, to see if they really are listening to what they most want to listen to! On such occasions I can give what seems to me to be a very creditable performance though all the time beset by the sneaking suspicion that the audience sitting out there in the darkness so scrubbed and clean and seemingly attentive might very well prefer to be listening to or watching something entirely different.

These small concert halls and the traditional organisers of the concerts have many things in common the world over. The organisers seem particularly in the New World to love heavy velvet hangings – the perfect ruination of a decent acoustic. And they are often proud to say that they have a Steinway, which simply means that they have a piano called a Steinway. The said instrument may not have been looked after or regulated or tuned or adjusted, or even played, for a decade. I wish that every hall had an acoustical shell and that velvet hangings could be a thing of the distant past.

This leads me quite naturally to my thoughts on the ideal hall. I suppose all artists have an ideal acoustic. All artists very often have to play in unsuitable and unpleasant halls. Ideally, my perfect acoustic would give the sound a certain sheen. The sound should have a resonance, a little echo, enough to make it reach the ears and the hearts of the audience without effort or strain. Halls that are acoustically dead are very difficult to cope with. It's no good in such places trying to force the tone. Perhaps the best thing is to hold back, to play at a whisper, to vary the tone as much as possible and to play with accuracy, assurance and attack.

CHOOSING YOUR PARENTS:
A YOUNG VIOLINIST'S GUIDE

One of the greatest problems in the infant violinist's life is the choice of parents and thereby his choice of faith. Despite the links and associations between the Christian and Jewish religions, we have as yet comparatively few virtuoso Christian string players and fewer violinists.

Could it be that the many Jewish and Russian Jewish violinists were produced by their aspiring parents out of a kind of collective grief – for assuredly the societies from which many of the best fiddlers come cannot be said to be happy – and that this led to a contagion of determination on the part of those parents that their offspring should prevail and prosper?

For my part, I was treated as a gift from above – but, far from being taken away to the monastery, my parents acted in lieu of the guardian monks of Tibet who rear the Dalai Lama. Whenever my mother was asked from whom I inherited my musical talent she would say, 'King David' – and perhaps the real genetic legacy derives from the finely tuned melodic harp (oldest known specimen in Egypt around 2000 BC), rather than from the thundering gongs (also tuned) of Tibet!

Be that as it may, parents play a great part in the development of a child musician (witness Suzuki's mother-tongue method with its insistence on the very active role of at least one parent). Verily – as the sacred admonition would say – the parents' role is crucial; yet as with all really serious roles it should be handled lightly (like violin playing!).

Looking back upon my own experience and comparing it with various others, my parents acted as mind and emotion stretchers and provided a background of total loyalty and devotion to each other and to their children. Music was by no means the exclusive concern of our family life and because as a family we had other interests, this was the important counterweight to the all-absorbing passion which my violin playing represented for me.

My private life was my music; and yet, by fruitful contrast, family life was a constant discussion of political, social and historical issues in which my father was deeply involved. My mother looked to my languages, engaged teachers, organised excursions. My father's addresses 'to the world' were marked by terrifyingly high moral principles.

But precisely such an intense moral focus made for difficulties. Our lives were generally assumed to be led according to moral precepts which, in their turn, created tensions which did not appear capable of resolution. Eventually we children came to recognise the reality of mortal frailties, and growing out of the parental nest – which had become something of an aviary – my sisters and I flew into the great boundless unknown. Looking back I have the image of two intensely good people, giving of themselves as very few modern parents would (perhaps sensibly) to their children, and, in retrospect, this picture takes on a deeply moving, very touching quality.

Even so, the bane of young violinists – or prodigies

as they were somewhat dramatically or sensationally dubbed in my day (today they are simply genetically gifted children; and even that description I find unnecessarily exaggerated) – is the ambitious parent. Whether it is better or worse that they themselves be musicians is a moot point. Good musicians, good instrumentalists, can be a blessing or a curse. In the best cases, musician parents continue to grow in depth and achievement with their most talented offspring and the reciprocal love, devotion and service continues.

There is no doubt that in all cases a full emancipation is essential and required by the child before he can arrive at that adult and mature period in which fulfilment, gratitude and satisfaction are united in equal degree, and when, as in my case, a very close and humane understanding, both respectful and thankful, binds the generations. In saying this, I draw not only my memories of childhood. After all I am now myself a musical parent. I am thinking of my son, Jeremy, an outstanding musician and pianist, with whom I am, as it were, on the very same wavelength and of whom his mother, Diana, and I are modestly proud.

Exercises: 3

PAINTING

What I call painting is an exercise which brings us nearer to the action of violin playing. Playing the violin involves carrying both arms as if they were nothing at

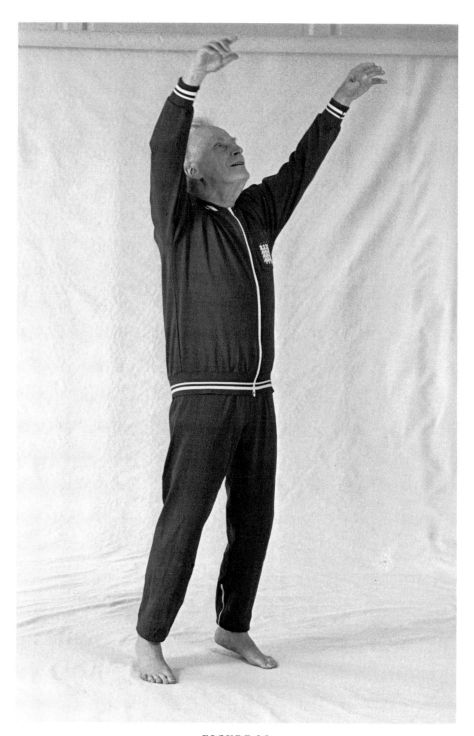

FIGURE 20

all. I think many people do not realise that it takes considerably more art and skill to play the violin lightly than it does to play it loudly. Indeed, the best possible training for young violinists consists in learning to play pianissimo and without pressure. Use of pressure discourages appreciation of subtlety, refinement and the infinite gradations of tone and nuance of which the violin is capable.

To start painting hold the arms out in front of you, allowing the hands to hang. Lean forward slightly and let the hands begin to circle in a natural motion – moving in opposite directions. You can make the circles as small or as large as you like by simply building on the motion that is already taking place. Let the hands move freely, swinging from the wrists.

Now begin to straighten the back, vertebra by vertebra, continuing the circles with the hands and carrying the arms upwards (20). As the arms move up the head also lifts, until it is as if you are painting the ceiling – hands stretched up and head tilted slightly back. Even the body tilts slightly backwards. The chest opens and the arms go right back. Keep the circular motion going. After a few moments stop and return the hands to your sides.

THE GOLF SWING

This is an exercise to encourage freedom of movement, balance and flexibility. Stand with feet comfortably apart, weight evenly distributed. Hold one arm out to the side at an angle of about 45 degrees from the body, hand relaxed. Let the other arm hold an imaginary

68

FIGURE 21 ▶

violin. Shift all the weight of the body onto the leg nearest the outstretched arm (**21**), then pivot round onto the opposite foot, swinging the outstretched arm round and still holding the imaginary violin in the other (**22**).

Repeat the exercise in the opposite direction, and do it on alternate sides as often as you like.

WORKING BEHIND THE BACK

This is an exercise to encourage flexibility in the shoulders, back and wrists. It is not easy, but with determination – or natural suppleness – it can be done.

Raise the right arm into the air straight above your head, keeping it against your ear. Then bend it so that the hand reaches as far down your back as possible.

71

◀ FIGURE 22

FIGURE 23

Bend the left arm upwards behind your back until the fingers of both hands grasp each other (**23**).

THE FIDDLER'S PRAYER

Place the tips of your fingers and thumbs together behind your back, and turn the hands inwards and upwards, bringing the outer edge of the hands against your back. Then close the fingers and press the hands together (**24**). Push the hands as far up the back as possible. This is good for the wrists.

FIGURE 24

FIGURE 25

SHADOW FIDDLING

It is important to be aware of your bodily image and of
the space which you embrace when playing the violin.
After all the foregoing exercises you should now be thoroughly loosened up, and ready to take up the bow –
first of all an imaginary one, then the real thing. (It is
easier to become aware of your movements when not
actually encumbered with bow and violin.)

Stand with feet comfortably apart, weight evenly distributed, and take up the playing position. Relax your
shoulder blades. Begin to stroke your imaginary violin
(**25**). The sensation should be very delicate and you

should be aware of the gradually expanding distance between your shoulder blades. Your back should be as sensitive and alive as your front – one plays with the whole body. The arms are open in an embrace.

Now take up the bow. Embrace as much space as possible in the circle made by your arms. Try to deepen the space between your shoulders. Balance the bow in the cleft of thumb and forefinger of the opposite hand, and stroke away. As you move the bow forwards you should feel the shoulder blades separating, the space between them increasing and deepening. As you relax into the downbow the shoulders fall and tension flows out of you. Check your fingers holding the bow – there should be as much space as possible between them.

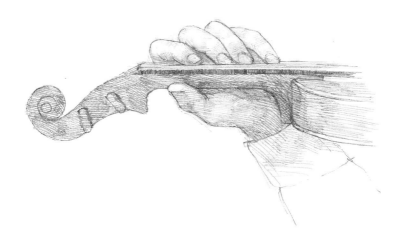

On composers and performance

A great work is a unity, and there is a key to the structure of the piece just as there is to its melodic and harmonic content. And there is a style which must characterise interpretation. By this I don't mean that there is only one way to interpret a piece of music. But there is a style, one style better than others, which allows the piece to breathe in its own particular way. Let me take an example: the operatic Italian style of Paganini demands flexibility of tempo, together with an almost exaggerated pathos. It requires that certain important notes be held, it requires an element of display, of showing off. The soloist keeps the audience hanging, as it were, on a breath. In this it resembles the style typical of much Italian opera, where the melody is supreme and requires the accompaniment to be adjusted to suit it.

We can contrast this with much of Schubert's music, which depends to a large extent on an even pace, almost unaltered throughout the piece. In Schubert the music is bound to the accompaniment. The melody must never dawdle beyond the stretch of the faster notes of the accompaniment, whether in a fast or a slow movement.

BEETHOVEN

In playing Beethoven the violinist should be a medium. There is little that is personal or that can be reduced to ingratiating sounds, pleasing slides and so on. Everything is dictated by the significance, the weight, structure and direction of the notes and passages themselves. Even the simplest phrases, those which seem little more than scales and arpeggi, reveal their supreme importance once it is realised how crucially they reside within the scheme of the particular work being studied. It is a form of holy communion in which all that is you – desires, appetites, frustrations, ambitions – is expunged, and another you is revealed, equally intense and yet somehow depersonalised.

Then, too, it should be remembered that Beethoven is not primarily a composer for the violin; he is a keyboard composer. For violinists, portati or slides must be almost totally banished. The tone must be pure, avoiding a throbbing vibrato.

In many important respects, Beethoven is not a romantic composer. He precedes that self-analysing, self-torturing, egocentric romanticism with which he is sometimes too closely identified. His music can be intensely dramatic, but he speaks for human kind and not for himself. Indeed, he achieves the transcendence of his personal suffering precisely because he is speaking for all. He rides a greater rhythm than his own and therefore in his violin concerto, for instance, the rhythm precedes the first bar. If Beethoven is played without thought, symbolism and supreme awareness, his music is drained and cheapened and reduced to noisy formulae.

I would like to suggest that Beethoven evolves a melody by process of deduction rather than by embellishment. The sign or symbol of his music has become universal, as have the Cross, the pyramid or the triangle. With Beethoven, as with Shakespeare, the thought is so perfectly couched, so simple, that it cannot be communicated more clearly, concisely, any more perfectly, or more beautifully. Therefore, the supreme importance of recognising in Beethoven, not the unrestrained romanticism of popular legend but this intense, compact, crystallised essence.

MOZART

There is no affectation and hypocrisy in Mozart. A healthy sense of humour, a rumbustious vulgarity as revealed in his letters, certainly a store of health and normality, more than sufficient to fuel an intensity of output of the highest and most expressive human significance. As my great teacher, Enesco, used to say, Mozart's music is a vineyard growing on the slopes of a volcano. There is not a note, a gesture or a syllable (and all three are synonymous in Mozart's music) which must not be turned to perfection. Yet within these notes, gestures and syllables there is, as there is in Shakespeare, all the human tragedy and comedy, sensitive commentary, passion and despair. Yet all sufficiently contained so they never break the formal code of conduct and elegance to which his age aspired.

Where Bach spoke for mankind, a voice communicating between humanity and God, Mozart spoke for the individual man and woman, spoke truly of the human condition. Yet the music is not self-tortured, not yet the prey to demagogues and uncouth tyrants, not yet reduced, as in recent years, by violence and despair, which hide and distort the wholesome and noble qualities of human kind. We will always return, if we survive, to the music of the great classical composers, to restore ourselves in body, mind, soul and heart.

BACH

Bach's music is more adaptable than any other to any idiom. Played by jazz groups, sung, whistled or blown on nose flutes, it would still be Bach and recognisably Bach. The only thing it does not stand is being sentimentalised or romanticised. Therefore the use of the piano, which is essentially a romantic instrument, presents problems. It must be used with discretion; and can be – as we witness in the recordings made by Glenn Gould. If the violinist should turn from the piano to the harpsichord as the accompanying instrument he or she will notice that he has totally to change his style of play. He has to return to a style of playing which is in fact much more authentic. It always takes me some hours to make the adjustment. With the harpsichord one has to play with an entirely different sound quality; one must forego intensity of vibrato and huge attack because this violates the code of that music which is dictated essentially by very deep faith. Always, the music of Bach resists such violent attempts to subvert it. Its intellectual complexity resists any attempt to manhandle it. Nor will it allow itself to be subverted in the other way, by being made too sensual.

When playing Bach, as in playing Corelli and Handel and Purcell, the sound must return to that quality one associates perhaps with choirboys: a high, pure quality. Bach, of course, was anything but a puritan – one should not confuse purity with puritanism. What Bach achieves is a sense of exaltation which is both continuous and permanent and which therefore goes beyond anything that we would describe as romantic. Take the introduction to the G minor sonata for violin alone, or the E minor movement in the E major sonata with harpsichord: these are sustained examples of a mood which continues throughout. How different from romantic music, where there must always be a contrast, a heroic and tender mood, an intense mood and a meditative mood, a joy and sadness. Bach sustains a mood for an entire movement. His time scale is different – as it is in all folk and medieval music and, for that matter, in the improvisations of classical Indian musicians expounding on a particular raga.

Although often extremely moving and passionate, Bach is not describing a personal passion nor trying to impose a personal conviction. He speaks for humanity and for timelessness: timeless love, timeless mind. Bach's mind can be compared only to a mind like Einstein's.

But the extraordinary thing about the music of Bach, or any of the composers of the classical period (I am thinking in particular of people like Corelli), is that the more the means of expression are restricted and clarified, the greater is the impact which the music has. In other words, I am saying that there is a paradox in the heart of playing such composers. The paradox is this. The less the performer or interpreter *tries* to interpret and to express feeling, the more feeling is in fact conveyed if – and here is the proviso – if the proportions are right and the quality of the sound and the interpretation is correct. And, of course, provided the interpreter possesses a sense of that extra-personal dimension.

The playing of Bach always seems to me the utmost test of a violinist's integrity. When I hear a violinist playing Bach and indulging in romantic fingerings on the G string for the sake of sound only, mixing the voices regardless of their contrapuntal individuality and producing a romantic effect which is not Bach's quality, then I realise they are on the wrong track, however well they play technically. They are taking away from the piece's integrity; they are bending the music to their personal expression, which prevents the universality of the work emerging.

HANDEL AND HAYDN

Handel and Haydn are always associated in my mind, perhaps because I see them both as reassuring composers. Of course they were deeply religious, and no doubt this has something to do with it. I always feel their music reveals no sense of doubt; it possesses a sense of utter and complete purity and an assurance that sits happily within its own age. It is music, it seems to me, always in the best of health and of few shadows – music which is life-giving and wholesome. This liberated, healthy spirit makes its own special demands upon the violinist when he approaches the music of Handel and Haydn, demands which the romantic violinist not sufficiently relaxed in mind and heart may find it difficult to meet.

BLOCH

Bloch composed Jewish music. When one says 'Jewish music' in this sense, we refer to sacred traditional music, to the intoning of the hazan in the Temple, which is something going back thousands of years, or to the liturgical music of the synagogue. But it relates also to another kind of 'Jewish music', which is for the violin and which is no less of a singing music. I refer to music for the violin as it was influenced by the gypsies in the south of Russia and Poland. This violin music has a strong Slavic, gypsy tinge. These two strains, the sacred and the folk idiom, were incorporated into Bloch's music. The earlier form marks his modal tastes. In fact he said that when he wrote modal music everyone accused him of composing Red Indian music. It may be possible that Bloch also thought it Red Indian because he had spent some time with the Indians of Arizona, I think it was, and New Mexico.

Bloch had the same instinct as Bartok, which was to

83

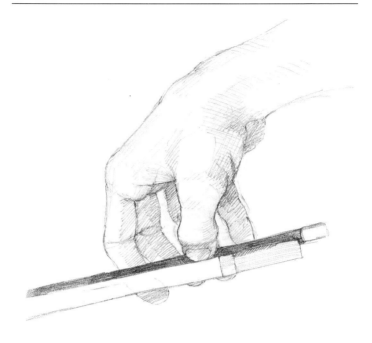

seek out roots, to seek out the authentic springs of
human nature. It is something, I suppose, of a modern
quest to conduct the search amongst peoples whom one
feels are not corrupted or tainted by modern civilisation.
All that notwithstanding, Bloch remains essentially a
Jewish composer, in his feeling for the Jewish cry of
despair, and of prayer and in his sense of the modal.

Bloch is the most famous of Swiss composers and always returned to his native Switzerland each summer,
where he took the most wonderful photographs – mainly
of himself against the rocky mountains, a prophetic
image. He was, incidentally, one of the first photo-
graphers to make use of the Leica camera. He had a

developed sense of the dramatic. He would take photographs by remote control in which the image of his astonishingly Old Testament face appears in front of the Matterhorn, seeming to be chiselled out of the same rock. This suggests self-aggrandisement, but in fact he was a most humble worker. When he was already a man of some years, in the early 1930s, he showed me some exercise books, handwritten note books, in which for two years he had deliberately done exercises in counterpoint, in many-voiced fugues, just to develop his hand and his ear.

His music is very largely a series of statements and meditations. I became acquainted first with the late composition *Baal Shem*. He also wrote a wonderful piece for me when I was a little boy of about seven or eight. It was called 'Avodah' and was the first piece of music I ever played by a living composer. He was a soul animated by the religious sense and no one wrote better for the violin. He ranks for me among the greatest composers for the instrument: Bach, Bartok, Enesco.

DEBUSSY

He is a most convincing genius, always utterly original, his mind moves along paths which are unpredictable and yet totally right. Debussy's music is carried on waves of subjective impulses. In visual terms his compositions reflect, in mercurial shifts of perspective, the play and motion between light and air and water.

Not for him the long unbroken line, the unity of pace and form of a great Schubert and Beethoven symphony. Notwithstanding, the design is perfect and inevitable,

85

with each individual mosaic, in that most feminine, impetuous and contradictory play of impressions and reactions, finding its place.

BARTOK

One cannot bargain with Bartok. One cannot say to the music 'I will make a deal with you – if you treat me kindly I will do the same for you.' In Bartok there is a note of fierce pride. I hear it at the beginning of the B minor violin concerto, or even, indeed, in the quieter sections of the second movement's theme and variations. There is no question of being able to make this music any more palatable, attractive or easier to play, by playing it slower, more sweetly, or adding a few slides to make it more ingratiating. At the same time it is not stark, naked and severe music; it is passionate music, but with a passion totally lacking in sentimentality, and with a sense of uncompromising integrity. Bartok's compositions are distinguished by an enormous intellectual content, an assured use of folk and feudal devices, and a musical imagination and command of note sequence, which shows up the melodic rigidity of the twelve tone school of composers. Yet along with his fierceness, his Hungarian intractability, there is an infinite melodic serenity. His is music which goes beyond the human, which reaches into heaven and hell. Perhaps this is because his music is so deeply rooted in the folk songs and culture of his land and carries the indomitable heritage of aeons of time. It is not merely the expression of one man but the expression of generations. It carries the affirming qualities of the universal spirit of man: defiant,

86

often uncompromising. It has humour, pathos and above all it has compassion. It sometimes seems to me that Bartok and Beethoven have much in common. There is a characteristic interplay in their string quartet writing between the tangible and the abstract. Both delight in sudden attacks, in pregnant pauses, in encompassing violence in serenity.

Bartok's mind turned quite naturally to music, as any Hungarian's might. But he also possessed an intellect equally powerful in matters of analysis, linguistics and botany, in which he excelled. And what is more he combined the intuitive sense with the intellect in a quite astonishing way, operating, it seems to me, on a higher level of intensity than any other composer I have ever met. For however much he commanded his medium, it was never without an intuitive grasp. By that I mean it was not solely intellectual. Bartok's grasp was always immediate, sure, exact: an instantaneous perception of what was right for the composition, for the music. I think he showed the same quick, sure approach when he stood up for matters of principle or against those who opposed him, as the Hungarian regime did. He left Hungary and went to America.

Of course the price of being uprooted was very great. Bartok had acute sensual gifts; his sense of smell and observation were as good as that of any Red Indian. The effect of this was to make him recall his beloved homeland with painful sharpness and clarity. One of his last offers of appointment in America was to study the north-western Red Indian tribes on a grant from the Northern Western University in Seattle. What an inspired move that would have been! He would have been in his element. I think the wild forests of that part of the world would have perhaps replaced Hungary and the Balkans which he so missed. And I think, too, it would have been a wonderful counterbalance to the world that he had known. I sometimes think he would have articulated for the Red Indians a musical language which in turn would have become universal. I have often maintained that every indigenous culture needs its Bartok.

ENESCO

Very many years ago, when I was first starting out, I remember Enesco taking me to the Colonial Exhibition in Paris. He made me listen to Balinese music, and to records of African music which absolutely fascinated me. What more could a boy of eleven or so ask for?

As a boy, one of the pieces which most appealed to me was Enesco's third violin sonata, composed in the popular Romanian style. I had a powerful urge to play gypsy improvised music when I was a boy, though I was trained in a way far too classical and too traditional ever to be able to improvise. I could only impersonate the gypsy violinist if I had a text and were given a role. Enesco's third sonata for violin and piano is, beyond its wonderful musical content and structure, a notational masterpiece. It provided the text I needed. Both violin and piano, by meticulously following the indications, give a convincing impression of gypsies unleashed. My darling sister Hephzibah and I revelled in it all our lives. But beyond this exuberant indulgence, Enesco was a very great composer, evolving an idiom all his own in his opera, chamber music, songs, in an extremely original harmonic structure.

Enesco was that very special mixture of human being which occurred in Vienna: early folk and gypsy roots from Hungary and Romania blended with the cultivated world of Western Europe. That is what gave rise to the incredible musical wealth of Vienna. Enesco partook of this inheritance, as did Bartok. Enesco was an extremely polished, refined and educated human being and musician. To him one can truly apply the term 'aristocrat'. Enesco knew the classics and the moderns and really had a tri-cultural foundation. He had his own Romanian style. As the French slopes will produce inimitable wines, so the Romanian hillsides produce their own distinctive music. Enesco had this and had, besides, grafted onto these roots, the best of the Germanic tradition which was available to him in Austria. Thirdly, he had the most cultivated French connections in Fauré, d'Indy and all of that world of French impressionistic, cultivated and highly sophisticated music. The combination of these three strands is absolutely unique. Enesco has the Debussian touch along with something of Brahms, shot through with Romanian vitality. We discern in Enesco a great intensity of improvised musical expression which, combined with his classical training, made him a powerful musical force. He knew most of the repertoire by heart. He always played from memory. He had an unerring sense of style and he conveyed a sense of improvisation even when playing a recognised piece by Bach. One always had the feeling that he could well have composed that music himself.

ON BRITISH MUSIC

English music and the English musical scene embodies a paradox, it does produce a recognisable style and yet in a way it can be said to follow none at all, or rather to open itself generously to a variety of international musics, artists, composers and practising orchestral musicians. It welcomes them all as it once welcomed Haydn and Handel – only two of the most notable examples. The English have a great sense of style of their own, as you can see in all the traditional ceremonial rituals, and also an intuitive sense of where that style leads, rejecting what is not in harmony with their natural habitat. They are drawn to the moderate and attenuated. But they are at the same time, despite this middle-of-the-road approach, far more able to respond and adapt to foreign styles. Furtwängler said he would rather conduct *Tristan* with the Philharmonia Orchestra than with the best German orchestra. The way that Beecham conducted Mozart also displayed this intuitive sympathy, which springs from a very fine sensitivity and a readiness to understand the other fellow, to give him the benefit of the doubt, to try to find the language that suits the style. By contrast more strongly flavoured national styles of particular cultures, such as the French perhaps, or the German, will often result in a summary rejection of something which is not their own.

It seems to me that sexual passion is very often lacking in English music. It takes as its great themes the glory of the state, or of God or of the church, or of the countryside even. But it seldom takes human passion as its theme. The great passions in English music are somehow more abstract – in this sense they display an almost medieval sense of mysticism and philosophy together with a worldliness almost Jesuitical in its detachment.

Of course there are glorious exceptions. Walton is one. Walton was a frank and unabashed sensualist – which is what more refined and intellectualised contemporaries reproached him with. However, one should not do his intellect an injustice, he was English after all, and that means he had as his background the choir school and the organ, which is essentially an intellectual instrument.

ELGAR

The whole point about Elgar is his Englishness, that inborn flexibility, subtlety, capacity for adjustment. Elgar to some extent reminds me of the English weather, which is so varied and can change in a few minutes but never goes to extremes, being always tolerable, never demanding arctic or tropical clothes. In its rich variety of tone and colour, it is like the many subtle shades of green you find in the English countryside. His music also expresses great nostalgia. One could almost say that Elgar's music remembers England, a beautiful green island, from a distance, from a point of exile, from the point of view of thousands of expatriate Britons who hold this sort of picture of it.

There is a tide in Elgar's music, a continuous ebb and flow, almost from bar to bar. There is nothing erratic in it, nothing that stops the flow. Elgar's music emerges, as it were, from beneath the surface; it flows without restraint, though there is control within it. There is a natural nobility in Elgar; his music is never crude, never aggressive, never vulgar. His climaxes have a kind of gentleness in them, even those that are most loud and violent. Although this sounds paradoxical I know that those who listen carefully to his music will understand what I mean. Sometimes these high dramatic moments even have a certain humour in them. Thus they are redeemed from being merely the expression of overwhelming power or determination. I believe, too, that there is nothing jingoistic about Elgar's music even though it was composed at the height of British power, there is nothing superior in Elgar's music.

Elgar wrote some of the most charming salon music and at the same time had a sense of grandeur, a deeply mystical belief. He was a fervent Catholic. Elgar's very Englishness drew on a more abstract basis of inspiration, it was both mystical, and then again imperial and, of course, to some extent deeply rural. But Elgar's sense of the country differed substantially, it seems to me, from other European composers of his time. Perhaps historical and political reasons can account for this. The elegance of Elgar's music reveals a world which was some distance away from the almost feudal world whose influence was still very strong in nineteenth-century Europe. In the England of Elgar's time the peasantry was already emancipated to a degree unknown in Europe, certainly in Central Europe, owing to the industrial revolution having begun far earlier here than elsewhere. And I think that the last vestiges of a true folk idiom in Britain had given way to rural middle-class, a phenomenon which was scarcely to be found in Eastern Europe, where a peasant still remained a peasant and no ameliorating presence had been introduced between the peasant and the feudal power. Thus Elgar writes at several centuries remove from the earthy roots which fed Austrian and Germany society and the great composers who wrote for it.

Yet when one talks of Elgar's essential Englishness one should always remember his affinities with the German school of composers and the fact that his harmonic idiom was essentially European. This becomes apparent as soon as Elgar is compared with other European composers.

With Vaughan Williams and Delius their harmonic idiom is a very personal one, their counterpoint and their measures are much closer to medieval music, as is also the case with Purcell. In these composers the phrase makes nonsense of the bar line, the phrase goes across it, cuts across it at various points; the phrase, in other words, is not tailored to the bar. Elgar's measures, even though they are much more free and fluid than the German style, are still none the less recognisably 'measures'.

PAGANINI AND THE MODEL OF THE MALE VIOLINIST

Paganini was a comet in the firmament of music. In consuming himself in the course of a life tragically curtailed by disease, he left meteoric treasures of spellbinding brilliance, compositions so dramatic in their Italianate operatic utterances, so technically exacting in their fashioning and execution, that even today a violinist, doing justice to their intrinsic worth, dazzles and transports his audience. He was the first prime example of the more than successful itinerant virtuoso, the commercially sophisticated, modern equivalent of the gypsy violinist, urban and urbane, far removed from the night encampment and long treks into the unknown; a man whose fascination and hold upon his audiences have hardly faded since his death in 1840.

Again I return to this question of style which the violinist who interprets Paganini must clarify. He must find the style which allows the piece to breathe in its own particular way. The operatic Italian style of Paganini demands freedom, together with an almost exaggerated pathos, it asks that certain important notes be held, it requires of the soloist an element of display; the audience is kept hanging, as it were, on a breath. In this it resembles the style of Italian opera, where the melody demands that the accompaniment be adjusted to suit it.

The legend of Paganini, the demon fiddler, though no doubt much embroidered, embodies a truth about, and a model of, the solo violinist as a dashing romantic figure. This is attested to by histories of unsuitable attachments, not infrequent among violinists.

But perhaps one of my favourite anecdotes about Paganini concerns his approach to practising. It seems that one day a patient, determined follower of the artist, eager to discover the secret of the master's technique, peered through the keyhole when Paganini locked himself away to practise. And what did he see? Paganini took the instrument from the case, put it up to play and then a little while later he put the fiddle back in its case. The story pleases me because it supports a theory of my own – there is such a thing as silent practice!

94

ON THE VIOLINIST

The violinist is that peculiarly human phenomenon dis-
tilled to a rare potency – half tiger, half poet. The violinist is an incarnation of a very specific animal agility in
the service of a singularly human transfiguration. It is
up to the violinist to speak of human memory, feeling
or thought; the violinist makes such intangibles palpable
by expressing them in sound and in rhythm. It seems to
me that the violinist must possess the poet's gift of pierc-
ing the protective hide which grows on propagandists,
stockbrokers and slave traders, to penetrate to the deeper
truth which lies within.

What in the tiger is compulsory is also forgivable,
understandable, because its tigerishness is not a matter
of choice. But when the tigerish becomes addictive and
obsessive in a human being it is because a deliberate
choice has been made. It is not enough to be favoured
in a particular way by hereditary factors, by birth and
environment and say 'that's what made me a violinist',
the true violinist, like the true mountaineer or astronaut,
is, I believe, largely *self-made*.

Thus, once committed, one's choice of creative activity
becomes the measure of all other occupations. Everything one does, thinks, feels, all one's senses of touch,
sight, of balance and motion, the manner of approach
to work and preparation, one's diet, even one's pleasure
and pains, are evaluated and proportioned in terms of
that singular creative aspiration which is both one's
own self-expression and, I believe, a mirror of mankind. I should rather say an X-ray scanner, since the
mirror, however valuable for self-discovery and analysis

95

is merely a reflector, but the scanner reveals profound lesions for the purposes of trying to heal them.

If I were asked to define artistry I would say that it is a subtle reaction to barbarism and crudity. By that I mean that in social or national or tribal division and strife, what one finds is imbalance, discrepancy. What one finds in music on the other hand are infinite subtleties, sensitivities and an infinite number of gradations, controls, checks and balances. Perhaps it is not difficult then to see why I chose music. It seems that our general reactions to violence and barbarity are to respond in kind, measure for measure, tooth for tooth, eye for eye, in retaliatory blind reaction. Art, true art, opposes such reactions in the way that I suppose real religion would oppose them, and teaches instead humility, tolerance, honour, respect. Open-mindedness and sympathy are the keys to understanding, to subtlety of feeling and reason, whereas condemnation and violence are the antithesis of understanding. In fact they only harden prejudice, hatred, factionalism and dissent. It always seems to me that the general principles that apply to what I suppose I might call enlightened human behaviour also apply to violin playing. Therefore I look upon music as the most complete exposition of the body and spirit of man – and of our universe.

In thinking of my life as a musician I feel I have every reason to be the most grateful man in the world. Certainly music has saved me many a time. Certainly without that sounding board, which is my work, life itself might have destroyed me. In many ways I owe my education to the violin, or at least to learning to play the violin, and that is why I am convinced that everything that contributes to a better performance on the instrument is also valid for life in general. There is simply nothing about making music that isn't applicable universally, that doesn't make for a better understanding, whether of emotion or of analysis or of psychology or of intellect or of human spirit.

What does music give me? It gives me a language which is in some ways more precise and more emotionally certain and more revealing than words can ever be, unless they are words used by great poets. What I have, what I feel I have, is a vibrating bond with my fellow men and women, a vibrant connection with everything that vibrates. For me, then, music is very much a meeting with and in a common humanity. I should also say that music has provided me with a constant opportunity of escape, because not all meetings are desirable or very welcome. Above all, my music has kept me moving. It has even kept me free. I remember how I was drafted into the American army in the very last few months of the war and fortunately was not required to report for the war was over. But during those war years I was able to do my war work voluntarily, travelling, playing everywhere. I think no one held it against me that I didn't carry a gun.

ON INTERPRETATION AND STYLE

Interpretation flows from a thorough understanding of the work. The musician, the performer, the artist must understand the work so well, or at least well enough, to feel not constrained but free. He must feel free precisely because he wants to be able to take freedoms with the work and not only permitted freedoms, if one can think in these terms, but all sorts of variations in bowing and fingering which help to serve this freedom. Free choice requires supreme assurance. This I believe is what the composer wants and needs. Let us take an example. Let us look for instance at a composer such as Alban Berg. Now what one sees written in the score is a portrait as it were of the music, a soundscape which Berg heard in his mind. But in order to bring about something approaching the ideal which the composer heard, the interpreter must often use totally different bowings and even fingerings in order to make that music come to life, to make it sound the way in which the music calls, to convey its essence. I am thinking now particularly of the Berg violin concerto where one is playing an intensely romantic, gesticulating, neurotic and very bittersweet piece. It is not enough, in other words, to say that music is expression. Of course it is expression, but the way in which that expression is created depends upon a host of factors, perhaps most of all upon the sorts of choices which the interpreter; the violinist, has to make. And it is the quality, the degree, the proportions of the interpreter's choice which gives us his style.

Style is the end result, the outward expression of the sorts of choices made. Let me take another example. The example of Kreisler. Who more perfectly represents the Viennese style? Who knows it better? But to know it takes a lifetime. It took me as long, in fact it took me far longer, to give one of Kreisler's Viennese waltzes elegance and charm than it ever did to learn to master a fugue by Bach. At seventy I at last seem ripe for both the ninth symphony of Beethoven and a Strauss waltz.

FIGURE 26

Exercises: 4

The point of the exercises we have done in preparation for taking up the bow and violin is to remind us of the interdependence of all parts of the body, and of how moving one will affect the balance of another. No movement happens in isolation, and my exercises aim to make us aware of the continual dance of energy which takes place within us, every bit as much as it does in the universe itself. They are directed towards sensing the

99

small movements, which are so important. It is not un-usual for people to think that big is better. Well, in many things it may be, but in the execution of music (and the musician is above all an executor) it is sensitivity to and perfection of the smallest details which counts. One needs to study and to understand the value of the small, the refined, the subtle – and its relation to the larger and more expansive effect or gesture. It is not enough for the violinist to be able to see what he or she is doing, it is necessary also that things be felt: much of the co-ordination of limbs and fingers, of head and feet, is in-visible and goes unnoticed unless we work to become more aware of it.

TAKING UP THE BOW

Take up the bow. It is absolutely vital to hold it as lightly as possible – rather as one might pick up a newborn bird: with exactly the same degree of sensitivity.

The index finger drives and guides the bow, so the knuckle of that finger must be particularly flexible (27). Opposite the index finger is the thumb, which rolls the bow. The third finger has a combined function: it balances to a certain extent and it also guides and turns the bow. In the photo we see it in its resting position, just above the nut. The little finger, of course, is the primary balancing finger.

The thumb is the pivot which works each of the fin-gers (28). There is a direct connection between it and each finger – they represent, as it were, centres of energy pushing in opposite directions, sometimes opposed and sometimes in harmony.

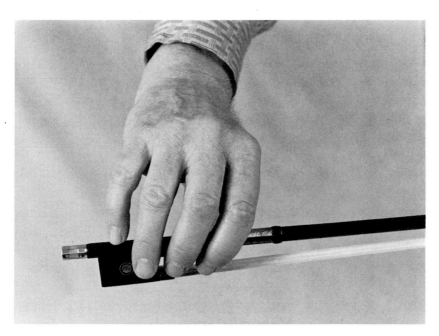

FIGURE 27

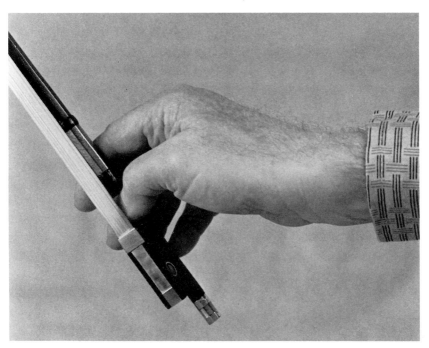

FIGURE 28

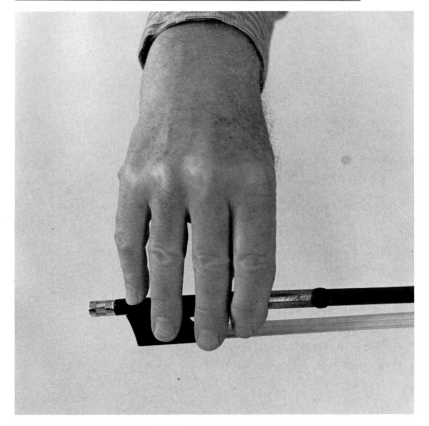

FIGURE 30

STRENGTHENING EXERCISES

Take up the bow. With your free hand hold it about half way along its length. Now use your bowing hand to drive the bow against the resistance of your grasp (**29**).

A useful exercise is to roll the bow with the fingers extended (**30**). Then roll it with the fingers bent (**31**). The angles of arm and wrist change accordingly. There

103

◀ FIGURE 29

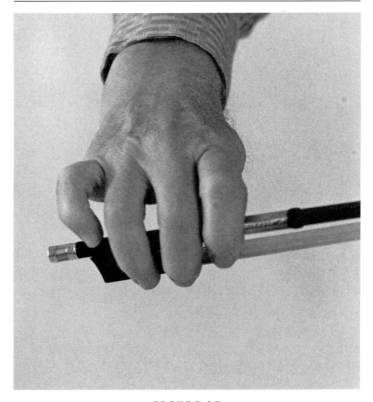

FIGURE 31

is no single motion which can be called independent; nothing in violin playing is isolated, everything is tied.

Make circles in the air with the bow. This can be done from the wrist, or the arm, or involving wrist, arm and shoulder.

Lift the bow from the horizontal by pressing down with the little, the balancing, finger.

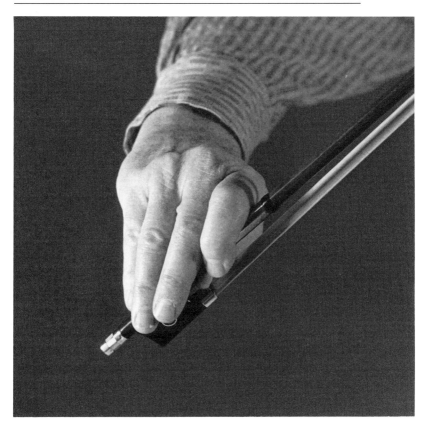

FIGURE 32

THE PUSH AND THE PULL

Observe the way the hand begins to slant at the beginning of the push, the upbow, by blocking the tip of your bow with your other hand (32). The position of the fingers changes according to the direction and force of the stroke. Notice the position at the end of a downbow (33).

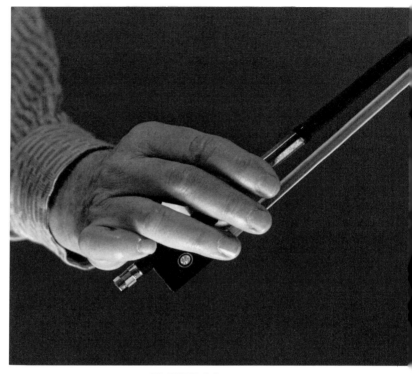

FIGURE 33

Both the up and the downbow should fulfil a natural inclination. The downbow describes a surrender to gravity – elongating the distance from spine to fingertips.

However, the upbow is also a surrender; try this yourself. Somewhere towards the middle of the upbow, a roundness in the back is felt, a feeling of embracing, of falling on a cushion of air, especially marked if you exhale as you make the upbow.

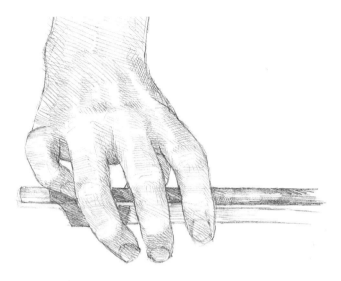

Fiddler on the hoof

Of course tails are *de rigueur*. Tails belong to the performance and no one can do without them or go anywhere without them, or if one does by oversight they must pursue one across half the world. The performing musician is as lost without his tails as he is without his instrument. But then comes the end of the performance and the tails are crumpled and sopping wet, and in a cold climate it is unwise to step outside while still wet. I always carry with me a large bag in which there is a change of clothes, strategically chosen for all occasions. I have an undershirt of wool for very cold weather, or cotton for somewhat milder climates, and then I have a black turtleneck pullover to which I can add a black cardigan. In this way I manage to look acceptably neat. Should I have to go on somewhere after the concert, to a party or a reception, I am equipped. My bag also contains a Thermos with herb or ginseng tea; or *molat*, an excellent powder, a rather superior kind of malted milk, containing all natural sources of strength and goodness.

Rehearsal clothes present similar problems. I prefer a shirt which does up at the collar and hangs outside the trousers, which does not need a tie and is very easy to put on. I find when I am working one does not want to be bothered with putting on ties and taking them off again. Shoes for the active and practising violinist are extremely important. The first rule is that they should be comfortable. Violinists stand for a great deal of the time. It is surprising how many of them forget this fact. I would recommend shoes which are flat and hold the foot. There is a German variety of sandal, which is flexible and enables one to stand for hours on end without becoming tired. Admittedly they are less good for actual walking, but then after all the violinist doesn't do much walking when he practises.

AGAINST DRINK AND DRUGS

I think it is most important to warn the performer against drugs or drink, or anything that provides an illusion of assurance. Such false comforters have proved the undoing of many a great artist. I always bear in mind what the porter in Macbeth said of drink – 'it increaseth the desire but taketh away the performance'. I commend that piece of wisdom to all violinists.

CONTENTS OF THE VIOLIN CASE

Nail-clippers, strings, resin, mutes – heavy and light – scissors, pincers, Kleenex, soft cloths, alchohol or metal floss for finger-board (leave tissue underneath because metal shavings otherwise fall over the violin), extra comb, pencils, family photos, special letters, good-luck tokens.

CRITICS AND THEIR USES

I think it important to cultivate an attitude of acceptance and even gratitude as far as critics are concerned. Hard though it may seem, I think one should do this particularly when they are negative and when they find fault. I think there is always a grain of truth in adverse criticism though that truth may not be what the critic suspects. In my experience, critics who give bad notices are generally wrong in their assumptions even if within their review there is an element of accuracy. In any event, it is far more profitable to apply oneself critically to one's work than to malign the poor critic. That is always a complete waste of time. If you feel you have been misjudged, it is better to avenge yourself on the stage by setting out to belie and disprove whatever it is he or she may have said about some performance. Of course it is pleasant to be praised, it is even pleasurable. But again this should not be taken at its face value. Criticisms, good or bad, are useful only insofar as they teach one something.

AN IDEAL HOLIDAY

A restorative holiday is one which corrects the imbalances of the 'regular' life. No one could possibly pretend that either an urban life, a continuously travelling life, or an executive musician's, is a balanced one. It may even be disastrously 'regular' – as is that of a drug addict, or as 'balanced' as that of a trapeze artist.

Balance requires an impossibly complete set of simultaneous conditions which, if theoretically possible, would be totally uneventful, supremely dull – and would probably drive us mad. (Imagine a life balanced as are a pair of scales.)

But an active balance of activities and leisure over a few months with sufficient carry-over so that memories, habits, stimuli overlap considerably – so that within one's inner being a certain equanimity is achieved; that is another matter!

Stress and strain require peace and quiet with unscheduled existence; a regular dearth of family time needs to be counteracted by essential time spent with one's family, free of other commitments and worries. It is good to satisfy the body, the skin's craving for sea water, sunlight, air, even rain, and experience a return to nature, bushes, trees, growing flowers and fruit. It is good to walk, sit, go barefoot on the bare earth; feel the cool evening breeze whilst watching the sun set against sea and islands; see the myriad stars overhead unmasked by electric light and pollution; greet the morning star at sunrise; satisfy the need for sleep until breakfasts creep back from noon to earlier hours.

In Mykonos I delight in simple tasks: bringing Diana

breakfast, shopping for fresh fruit, bread, vegetables, yoghurt, olive oil and the odd lovely surprise – ceramics, lavender plants. An ideal holiday will bring me to a different civilisation, language, customs – people who are different from those we normally meet, who are seldom aware that I play the violin.

I love walking, swimming, reading, making outings to the beaches or to lunch, and above all no telephone! Yet I confess that, belonging as I do to the greater world and still reading the London *Times* every day, it is almost impossible to cut myself off entirely, and the habit of dashing off a letter to the Editor – probably to remain unpublished – is one I cannot break.

After the first week or ten days, I love quiet daily work on the violin, generally from about five to dusk or sunset, one to two hours, looking out past a tall cypress and some vegetation, figs, cactus, pomegranate, vines, quince, bamboo, to the Aegean and Delos in the west, rather as I did as a child in San Francisco looking out over the Pacific.

Wonderful things begin to happen. A total closeness, reliance, dependence between two people, together at almost every hour, with many stimuli and distractions yet none that tear us apart from one another.

Reduced to basics – air, water, sun, rock, earth, heat, I make other discoveries – legs are stronger, posture better, muscles in feet, toes, chest and back are toned, tuned, resilient and eager. A newer and higher level of quiet, precise work – more specific – clearer in concept and execution – is the reward for unhurried, relaxed exploration with violin and bow.

Exercises: 5

PUTTING UP THE VIOLIN

Rest the violin comfortably on your shoulder, tucking it into the neck and keeping it slightly raised, not parallel to the floor (35). Now turn your head, raising it in order to lower the violin into the playing position. Then gently allow the chin to touch it (36). The violin is actually resting on the collarbone; the chin keeps it there, but without undue pressure. The chin should never be used to nail the violin into place. Experiment to see that the violin is firmly but delicately held by rotating it beneath the chin. Viewed from behind (37) it can be seen that there is space between the shoulder and the back of the violin.

At this point if you release your hold on the violin it will decline (38). It should not remain parallel to the

◀ FIGURE 34   ▼ FIGURE 35

FIGURE 36

FIGURE 37

FIGURE 38 ▶

floor. If it does, you are using too much chin pressure. Take your hand away gently and see what happens.

THE PIVOT OF THE ELBOW

There is a reaction in the shoulder when the arm pivots on the elbow. When the hand moves towards the body the shoulder goes to meet it; when the hand moves away from the body the shoulder falls away.

Try to feel this for yourself. Freely extend the arm; feel the weight in the shoulder. Now bend the elbow (39). The shoulder moves forward to meet the hand. In moving from one position to another, everything hinges on the elbow. It is important to be aware of what is involved in making the movement.

Now try the same thing, holding the violin. When the hand is in the lower position (40) notice how the violin is slightly raised and the arm freely extended. Move from a low to a high position (41). Since the violin is slightly

◀ FIGURE 39   ▼ FIGURE 40

FIGURE 41

raised, the hand is actually falling. Do you feel the
shoulder move beneath the violin? It is important to
realise that we play from height: moving the hand from
low to high positions is a sensation of falling, or throw-
ing the hand. We work with, not against, gravity.

ROLLING THE VIOLIN

This exercise has two objects: to make one adopt the
best position for the thumb and to prevent one's chin
from exerting too much pressure on the fiddle. We do
this by developing the rolling ability of the thumb. As
the violin cannot be rolled when clamped down too hard
by the chin, the exercise attains both objects.

Roll the violin between the thumb and each of the
fingers in turn, in a rocking motion (42). Notice the
position of the thumb supporting the violin – the violin
is resting on the last joint. Many violinists hold the

FIGURE 42 ▶

thumb too high, thus depriving themselves of the use of that joint.

Now take the neck of the violin between thumb and forefinger and roll it gently, keeping the chin free of the chin-rest.

Another fault is to let the thumb rise above the finger-board, and to clamp the hand too tightly. This immobilises the first finger. The correction position of the thumb preparing for the roll is shown in figure **43**. Here the second finger is on the G string, but the roll should be practised using each finger in turn in all positions on all strings.

REFLECTION ON HISTORY

Human history seems to be a record of a certain tenacious blindness fortified by prejudice, superstition and lethargy, very reluctantly giving way to light, to clarity, to what finally appears as the obvious. And when we do enjoy real enlightenment (or is it perhaps only the illusion of progress?) then much of our energy is dissipated in retaliation against those who have failed to recognise what we do, or are assumed to have impeded our forward thrust. Perhaps this explains the collapse of revolutions. The accomplishment sensed at having arrived at enlightenment, of having made progress, is dissipated by the energy spent on the guillotine 'correcting', as it were, the faults of others who have either not arrived at the same point of progress or who are seen to have prevented its attainment. The result is that those who led the revolution are only back where they started, sometimes even further back.

ON AMATEURS

I would hate to think that I am not an amateur. An amateur is one who loves what he or she is doing. Very often I'm afraid the professional hates what he is doing. So I'd rather be an amateur. And I would like to see a society in which music, as was the case in old Vienna, is played by everyone.

ON NOISE

We live in days in which every appetite is abused or exploited or commercialised, and now there is even music which masks the genuine article. There is music calculated to reduce our alertness, our resistance to buying in a store; there is music manufactured with the intention of numbing our senses, of depriving us of our identity or of lulling us into false choices. What is worse is that it becomes increasingly louder and our sense of hearing reacts by developing a kind of protective deafness. Just as a pair of hands grow calloused with heavy work, so deafness is our only defence against the relentlessly increasing decibels of our appallingly noisy environment.

STYLE AND THE VIOLINIST

Perhaps of all nations the English have the best sense of style because they can play convincingly any music from Purcell to Elgar; they can play the romantics and the classics; the pre-classics; they can play Monteverdi. In each case they seem intuitively to understand the right approach. Style is really an indefinable, subtle quality. When do you have it? When don't you have it? It's like choosing clothes. The trained eye knows that particular shoes go with a particular outfit or which set of colours ' go well together. It is in matters of style that the raw recruit is revealed. This is the same with violin playing as with anything else. With the violin this is the turn of a phrase, it's the right degree of vibrato, it's a question of taking the right precautions, observing the right changes in volume. It is a matter of restraint and also, of course, a matter of abandon. It is knowing when to do which. It is the little accent where it belongs, it is the twist of a phrase in terms of rhythmic inflections, it is the sense of bringing out of music what is in music, not imposing on it, not laying on it either something too grandiose or too pompous or an affected charm. It is simply finding out and sensing the true nature of the music and serving it.

NERVES AND STAGE FRIGHT

A state of nerves, fear before a performance, anxiety on the platform, a disabling tension – these are very common occurrences and I have felt them all. However, it is important to know that such an affliction is an end product, not a first cause. First causes lie far behind the final appearance of stage fright. We might list among the causes: technical, emotional and psychological reasons proceeding from inadequate preparation, fear of a lapse of memory, and perhaps certain irritations peculiar to different artists, nervous allergies, for example, or particular situations that put them off centre. Psychological reasons may stem from a sense of the occasion, combined with the desire to do particularly well, which is in turn undermined by the fear that perhaps this performance may not be all I know it can and should be. The last-mentioned is a persistent and probably a very salutary problem because it is exactly this which keeps us on the straight and narrow path. It is the obligation of the artist to take every possible precaution, to do everything that is humanly possible, to avoid letting down himself and his audience.

Let me consider these underlying causes of stage nerves. The technical problem is usefully considered first. Violinists, and certainly many people in other walks of life, know very well that at certain important points of execution, whether in their music or facing an expectant crowd, or perhaps even when quite alone yet expecting something of themselves, an awful feeling of inadequacy disables them. I have known the feeling many times and certain technical problems took me years to surmount. Others would yield one day and be difficult or impossible to achieve another day. But painful experience has taught me that as soon as a problem yields, even once, I need never lose heart because it merely remains to consolidate whatever it is that made it possible. This consolidation may require perhaps years of prolonged examination and analysing, but when you've done a thing once, you can do it again.

This element of faith in work over a very prolonged period is one of the most important efforts leading towards the solution of problems. There is, I believe, a Chinese saying to the effect that habit begins as a spider's thread and ends up as a steel cable. It is this elusive and almost intangible first sensation of something which is positive and which you know will lead on to the solid capacity which enables you to make light of difficulties. It begins with the intuitive ability to recognise and choose the right over the wrong. And how do you know the difference when preparing a piece of music? The right is always easier, the right is always more elegant, the right always is more coordinated than the wrong. It is a very simple yardstick. Though it is infuriatingly difficult sometimes to attain the lack of strain a good technique displays. The perfect juggler does his juggling act effortlessly. It not only looks effortless, the seeming ease is not misleading. To be sure a great deal of effort went into mastering the technique, but the whole object of mastering it is to render it effortless.

The violinist, concentrating on some deficiency in technique, recognises when a movement is smoother and can learn what makes it smoother. This happens when musician and music are joined in one even flow of body, mind, will and imagination in which everything is correct and continuous. There must be no impediment. If there is one joint that is not part of the flow, it will not continue to the fingers, nor will it continue back from the fingers into the mind for the control, or what we call the feedback, which is essential. This is quite obvious in a person who has a stiff knee or in a person who has a tennis elbow; the motion does not go through that joint smoothly. Thus, at every point in our daily exercises, we must choose between what is better and what is worse; that sensation we are looking for is smooth, where everything seems to fit into a rhythmic sequence and the flow is uninterrupted. One wants when playing or practising to have an idea of the perfect position of bow, fiddle and body; an idea of the perfect motion, the perfect ellipse or circle or of whatever it is we seek. When we have this picture in our mind's eye it will eventually produce its embodiment in our movements.

Emotional tensions on stage are more difficult to deal with. I have been through situations where I was worried about the health or safety of my wife or children, about not receiving a telephone call when I expected it announcing their safe arrival at a given place. I would be in a high state of worry and my mind could not concentrate. I have played the concert none the less, but my emotions were elsewhere. Of course, there are other, happier emotions that heighten one's capacity for playing in a positive way; for instance, when one is very young and first in love and wishes to play in such a way as to convey one's most intense emotions, wanting to convey as much of love as is possible.

There are some artists so completely at one with the music that the emotion stems from the work and not from any outside stimulus. This can happen when playing alone, or when reading a composition. The performer's job is to translate what he sees in a composition, the ideal image of the score, into sound. There is a wonderful chain of events that happens and reinforces the performance when everything is smooth and working well, when the act of interpretation creates its own momentum and the imagination is enriched by the very palette that one is using. It is a cycle which is benign and fructifying.

Emotions are the very life-blood of music and the very lifeline of communication, especially in the absence of words. It's the quality of sound, the inflections, the particular phrasing, that will make one phrase speak and another wooden.

The psychological reasons for nervous tension are to be found in the artist's temperament, his inborn antipathies to certain situations, in the feeling of loneliness on the stage, in assumptions of what is expected (sometimes false), in deeply felt fears, often misplaced, that the hall is not right, or the acoustics bad, or the critics are out front – all of these elements which are, in fact, irrelevant to the actual job in hand, to the calling.

There is no doubt, too, that the overwhelming desire to succeed may actually inhibit an artist's performance. The performer must give everything to the work; but he must not be dominated by it, he must not allow himself to be subject to one single exclusive dominant ambition or fear. That is going too far because it will end by strangling the very thing one wishes to achieve. We all need variety, change, stimulus and the opportunity for contrast, and I think that contrast is synonymous with the widest possible experience of the colours of music, of the musical palette. As soon as you know what the opposite is, it makes you stronger in your resolve and more clear in what you wish to achieve. Thus, having gone through the pain of technical insufficiency often, I know exactly what I wish to avoid. It may be that one sometimes possesses the genuine conviction that this is going to be the best performance in the world. Perhaps it is, and naturally one wishes to re-capture at every moment the perfection of that perform-ance. But, of course, it is not possible. Lucky the artist who knows that feeling once every ten times he plays a certain piece. Perhaps once every five, as one gets more masterly. With due preparation on tour it may be pos-sible to achieve it every other time, giving fine perform-ances on five or six nights in succession. But one must also be prepared to survive the disappointments and maintain inner and outer equilibrium. Every artist plays badly on occasion – the wise ones learn from experience.

I can remember an occasion when I played badly in Milan. It was early in our marriage. My wife, Diana, was feeling rather ill and we had had a dreadful summer trip on overcrowded Italian trains where everyone was eating salami and in those days there were lengthy delays at the borders. We finally arrived in Milan at four o'clock in the afternoon and were about to take a couple of hours rest before the concert when the telephone rang and the manager informed us that the concert began at five o'clock. There was nothing to be done. We dressed quickly and were dragged along to this awful stifling underground hall. I played Paganini so badly that only the haziest memories of that concert remain.

Of course we ran away from the concert as soon as it finished. No one really could honestly come backstage and say it was extravagantly beautiful or anything like that. They did pay the fee fortunately. In those days (and they still do so in Italy), they paid in cash. You received huge envelopes stuffed with lire. Really you had to take a small suitcase. Receiving a fee has never depressed me, although on that awful night I did not feel I had really earned it. None the less the better part of me knew that I should accept it. After all the audience had paid, so there was no reason for anyone to make an undue profit. And, what is more, I had suffered. I often feel that it is the artists who suffer who deserve the fees. If you play badly and you really have gone through hell, you deserve some sort of compensation. Whereas if you have enjoyed the concert and had a triumph, you really deserve it much less. With this reasoning in mind, I pocketed the fee and came back to the hotel with darling Diana and asked the porter if there was a train for Venice. There was. We took it and fled into the night.

A musician, a soloist particularly, lives on his memory.

Fear of occasional lapses of memory may be one of the chief causes of excessive nervousness on stage. All I can say is that everyone has such lapses. It has happened with me both when I have been playing a work I have just crammed into my head or equally with an old work that I have known many years and taken for granted. Suddenly there is this feeling of realising that you do not know it. Or suddenly you begin thinking that you really have no right to know it because you have not put in the required work, or gone over it sufficiently often in your head. You come to a point in your performance and think ahead and ask yourself – do I really know the next bar? Do I really know the notes I am going to play? That is enough to cause a very definite degree of nervousness.

Fickle though memory sometimes is, it is also an inestimable boon and comfort. One of the privileges of being a musician is precisely the fact that you can keep your mind occupied when other people cannot, or when others imagine that your mind is vacant because you are not talking. You can easily spend hours going through scores in your head and I find this to be a wonderful refuge and a quiet kind of mental discipline of the best sort in the world.

A classic example of the refuge I have in mind concerns the mother of Antal Dorati. It is one of the most wonderful stories I know. Near the end of the war she was rounded up with all the Jews in Budapest to be sent to the concentration camps. She was herded along with others into some wretched house in Budapest. By great good fortune the Germans were soon to capitulate and thus the Nazis were not finally able, in this particular case, to wreak their worst. However, she had to spend quite a number of days in that house while other women were going off their heads. In a terrible state of mental and physical anguish she kept her sanity because she knew all the Beethoven quartets by heart; she also knew each of the parts so she could mentally play through the violin parts, the viola part and the cello part and take strength and comfort from the discipline of doing so. She had been raised with music and this capacity for thinking through great and noble music kept her sane during those horrific days.

Among the tensions which may afflict the soloist I must mention exhaustion, more often physical than mental. Physical exhaustion in young musicians is one of the most prevalent conditions, as I know from my own experience. Children need a lot of sleep. Now my father looked after me most devotedly on tour and he never accepted more than one concert a week. None the less I remember at certain stages in my late teens there were certain occasions when I didn't get the sleep an adolescent needs. Once I even fell asleep on my feet during the second movement of the Beethoven violin concerto, in a concert I gave in Boston with Koussevitzky. There were other times when the sheer effort of facing a concert was more than I felt physically capable of doing and I remember reaching the end of such concerts in a state of very great fatigue, all the more so since at that time I was not conscious of the physical preparation required to prepare a large work for public performance. It is something I am all too aware of now.

I realise now that I did not know how to relax. For that matter, though I played the violin very well (the early recordings are testimony to that), I still did not know *how* to play it. So, it was always a matter of wanting and hoping to achieve something which could not always happen satisfactorily in a state of exhaustion. The young player is full of excitement, spontaneity and romantic feelings. That is the way of youth and that is how it should be. But such impulsiveness encourages one to do things that are not necessarily the best preparation for a concert. As I grew older I became interested in yoga and other exercises as a means of developing a feeling of inner calm. Solo performers as they grow older do find ways to pace themselves and conserve energy – or they will crack beneath the strain.

SOME WARMING-UP EXERCISES

Often when exercising it is a good idea to begin pianissimo and, as you warm up, grow louder by degrees. If you are in good form and playing well, these warming-up exercises may be continued for half an hour.

Try, for example, to maintain a soft, delicate feeling in hands, wrists and fingers. Try, also, to increase circulation by the compression and release of fingertip pressure. Both left- and right-hand fingertips should apply alternating and rhythmical pressures on finger-board and bow. The fingertips are applied across strings, up and down strings and in different combinations on the bow as well. This opens a new sensation for the violinist who has thought the fingers a solid mass, or thought them all of a piece, and exposes the value of each finger as it relates to the others. Press deliberately with the tips of the fingers in various combinations. Hold for a few seconds. Release.

Remember too that every upbow should begin with passive elongation of the fingers and a soft wrist. The downbow begins with passive, soft knuckles and fingers – above all, first finger and *thumb*.

With these warming-up exercises we combine breathing in rhythmically and *humming* as we exhale.

Perhaps the most important awareness of distinct parts of the body comes as we realise the different functions of collarbone and shoulder. The collarbone should provide a base for the violin, with the chin pulled back into the neck, but not pressing on the violin – while the shoulder remains free to adjust to the swing of the arm and the change of position.

A useful warming-up exercise with the bow involves huge, wide swings which describe a circle in the air, one arc of which is the length of the bow drawn over the string. Do it clockwise and you get exaggerated upbows. Do it anti-clockwise for downbows. Remember – *large* circles. And keep the bow arm moving. You will find your arms and chest visibly expanding as you draw the bow down, barely feathering the string. Keep the bow arm moving until it reaches far behind the back. The effect of this is to open the chest and give a feeling of exhilaration quite contrary to the crouching, clenching stance around the violin which is so often adopted. These wide movements can be done in various rhythms and combinations, on two, three, or four strings, and at different speeds, beginning on an up or downbow.

BOWING BUT NOT SCRAPING

When one considers the question of bowing, one undertakes an analysis of some subtlety for we dissect the movement into its component parts. There is not only an order, a sequence of *active motivation* where, for instance, the elbow of the right arm is the point providing the specific pull (and/or push) of the bow stroke, in down and up bows, always more or less smoothly (that is, accented as in martelé, or flowing as in détaché). This order is incorporated in a total body-supporting motion, however small – whether the original impulse comes from feet or head, through the waist and shoulders and finally into the fingers. But there is equally an order, a flow, or *sequence of relaxation* which proceeds from the fingers *backwards* into body. For instance, in the upbow movement, the fingers 'give' slightly and the elbow pushes; then, the wrist 'gives' (slightly) rising a little with the forearm, allowing the hand to fall; and *then* the sequence of relaxation flows from elbow and back along to shoulder. When bowing well it is impossible to 'jump' or exclude any of these sequential points.

These are subtle and delicate sensations. Always check that the neck is soft, that the breathing is easy, that the bow and the violin are balanced in the hands and the fingers and on the collarbone; see that the body is balanced on the feet and the whole body is poised, soft and yet alert.

Rhythmic pressures on bow strokes
Play continually with the elements of gravity, momentum, balance and weight. Always feel, search for and combine movements.

133

Proceed to separated strokes: short, long, martelé. Then lift the bow off the string at various speeds. Feel the point where the stroke is initiated; you may find the downbow begins at the elbow, or it could be initiated in the feet. Use the bow at different lengths, speeds, dynamics and, of course, on different strings.

Feel the loosening of wrist and fingers as the momentum of the stroke allows them to travel with the bow, passively in preparation for the next stroke. Feel the thumb solidify in its length to accept the greater weight of arm on bow. Feel the solidifying extent also of the hand and the wrist. Feel the rolling of thumb as it elongates. This happens sometimes when approaching the frog. On long strokes, undulating over two or more strings, apply the pressure accent sometimes on the lower, sometimes on the upper, string. Study the subtle and fine adjustments required in terms of the right arm level and the momentum at the change of a stroke.

Seek to keep the flexibility of both bow and fingers, even while exerting a resistance to pressure and to direction.

Bouncing exercises are most useful: one, two, three, four or more bounces on each stroke, in all parts of bow, all speeds, all strings, all dynamics. Sometimes on two strings alternately.

I believe the above suggestions are as important as playing études. Études are excellent when the body machinery is functioning; useless if it is not. Furthermore, under my regime, the violinist must continually concentrate on whatever he is trying to do because he is inventing his exercises. He cannot do them blindly or play them automatically from the printed page.

Now I am aware that I have placed a great deal of

emphasis on keeping loose and supple the wrist, elbow, shoulder, neck – indeed the body as a whole. But, having established one form of flexibility, the time has come to remind my readers, and myself, that vertical flexibility of the wrist in the bowing arm is all very well. But we must also concentrate on sideways-horizontal movements of the bowing hand.

So, then, with the fingers resting on the bow, begin compressing them with rhythmic pressures. This has the effect of delicately pumping blood through the fingertips. Fingertip pressure on the bow is coordinated with the same pressures of the left-hand fingers on the strings. By altering the shape of the hand holding the bow, *without* changing the position of the fingers, while playing a variety of strokes, we learn how the hand merely moulds, forms, reforms and focuses the directional energy arriving from the arm and beyond. We are here deliberately restricting vertical floppiness of the right wrist and concentrating on the sideways-horizontal movement of the hand and the many combination exercises to be derived from it. This will lend strength, stability and precision in spiccato and staccato.

Naturally the wrist in the horizontal strokes, though firm, is not rigid. The inside of the wrist and the base of the thumb (which is a crucial pivot) remains receptive to the momentum from the arm.

I believe it is possible for a violinist to command not only most styles of music but also most styles of playing. Some players are very strong and have apparently 'stiff' wrists. Others are more delicate and have 'soft' wrists. There is a time and a place for both and for everything in between.

FIGURE 44

Exercises: 6

APPROACH TO PRACTISING

Remember above all when practising the violin, that one is dealing with a living entity. This is a cardinal principle. In a sense it is true that we do nothing ourselves,

we are merely guiding a living force. We must be relaxed, we must be at one with the instrument, in harmony with it, in tune. Remember too the general principle that no part of the body is dissociated from the
commitment to playing. Every action has its reaction. It
is possible that certain parts of the body which are distant from the violin – the toe say, or the heel, may have
a very small degree of association with the main movement and are seemingly unrelated to the fingers' activity
on the finger-board. But, however small, there is movement, and that distant quiver is essential in bringing the
performer into harmony with his instrument. What I
look for is a sense of the organic whole, a readiness to
vibrate, a readiness to accept, a readiness to have faith
in the motion – to support it, to believe it, to accept it.
I quite deliberately touch on spiritual matters here
because I think that the feelings, the spirit and the
character all enter into this search for the perfect motion, which it seems to me is the aim of all good violinists. You must have faith in the motion and faith in the
continuity of the motion – faith that it will carry you
provided you go with it and not against it, and provided that through practice the trajectories along which
the motion flows are perfected.

The fingers must move between the lowest possible note
they can play and the highest with the help of both the
wrist and the pivot of the elbow. Starting with the hand

FIGURE 45

FIGURE 46

in the lowest position, play any note you like (**45**). Observe, once again, that the violin is not parallel with the floor but slightly raised, so the hand is going to travel *downwards* when it moves to a higher position.

Now move backwards and forwards between low and high positions, drawing the bow evenly across the strings (**46**). The movement should be fluid and graceful.

FINGER EXERCISES

It is as well to remember that the three basic violin motions, that is to say shifting, vibrato and trill, are intimately connected and are all produced by the same propulsion – the pivot of the elbow. In the trill the finger is thrown very fast, repeatedly, against the finger-board. With a fast trill the motion resembles that of the vibrato. Try it and see the connection for yourself.

There is a connection between practising the trill and learning to throw the finger properly, and likewise between correct finger movement and the ability to shift easily between one part of the violin and another.

Practise lifting and elongating the fingers in a variety of positions – e.g. in figure **47** thumb and middle finger oppose one another. When the fingers and the elbow reach the upper position there has to be a reaching out by the fingers – an elongation (**48**). Of course each finger must be capable of extension both singly and in a pair.

Lift all four fingers. This should be a deliberate opening movement in which the muscles involved are very active. The natural bias of the human being is to hold, to

139

FIGURE 47

FIGURE 48

FIGURE 49

grasp, to cling to things. But this involves tension – and tension shortens the muscles. The result is loss of flexibility, a holding back, a fear – which has a bad effect on the playing.

Let the fingers fall (**49**). The violinist should be the least grasping of creatures. He or she has to learn to give, to open, to lift.

These lifting and falling exercises, assiduously practised, will give a very resilient, spring-like action to the fingers.

141

FIGURE 50

SHIFTING

In figure 50 you see the elongated finger as the hand prepares to shift up the finger-board. Always check that the inside of the palm and wrist are loose. One way of doing this is to ask someone else to gently press on the wrist, checking that it will give.

A NOTE ON VIBRATO

The violinist must learn to control every possible nuance of tone. It is a question of sensitivity, of subtlety, of learning to know yourself. In the exercises pictured here we have been exaggerating the motions. As you know, in many cases these movements are so small that they may not be noticed at all. But they are there, as vibration at least. Ideally, when one plays one should feel in the right arm the vibration of the bow hair on the strings – a wonderful sensation. When you reach that degree of subtlety you will be holding the bow in such a way that the finger joints, the whole hand, is sufficiently light and delicately poised to sense those vibrations. The moment tension or hardness enters into the hand then of course the vibrations will not be felt – they cannot penetrate. These exercises of mine point towards the possibility of sensing and welcoming these vibrations.

REMEMBER... when practising with violin and bow always move from soft to strong, from pianissimo to fortissimo and from slow to fast by degrees, never the other way around.

IMAGES OF THE SELF: SOME FINAL THOUGHTS

This book represents a life-long search and, in fact, however protracted, a successful treasure-hunt. Many moments of apparent hopelessness – yet always the reward – and eventually the full and magic treasure-chest *inexhaustibly* rich. Some instrumentalists have known a form of perfection without search, having untroubled natures and perfect formations – yet for those who need help I would like to feel that my violinistic experience and my musical experience will encourage and bring hope and relief to countless of my younger colleagues.

It is essential that the working or aspiring violinist has a picture of him or herself as a player. In order to gain this portrait you may use a mirror (often useful) and your imagination to build an image of the self. Unless you know what the result of your motions and actions will be, then your progress will always be fraught with dangers. Of course this is not to say you may not succeed; you may strike the right note at once out of talent or desire. And if you have someone you are imitating then of course it will help. So desire, talent, ambition, the right teacher, all these things can carry the violinist for a while. But when the violinist is left alone all of that is going to collapse, and bad habits spring up, all too easily. So, in practising, it is your view of yourself which you must begin to establish in your mind. You must see the series of curves and circles out of which the ideal violinist is built.

By practising pianissimo we are carrying the bow. By carrying it we are judging its weight and learning the distance and the angles between the bow and the strings. We learn, as it were, to see with the body. How do I know that the bow is landing on the G string? It is because the bones and muscles and nerves of my arm take on a certain formation. It's not that I guide the bow down with my eyes. I KNOW. In the same way with the notes I play. My fingers become accustomed to the distances. My ear confirms that I am playing the correct note, F-sharp or E, but it is my fingers carrying naturally and easily without tension or pressure across the known distances that find the right note. It is unfortunately a great mistake of many teachers and parents, and many violinists, that they or their students work with enormous will, desire and courage – for perhaps ten hours a day – and force through an approach to a particular piece of music. As surely as they do this they defeat themselves.

To work with tremendous energy and dedication is of course laudable. But if you work with enormous will and desire and courage for anything up to ten hours a day then the tension intrudes upon the work and will take away from the purity of proper learning. You must work with lightness, with ease. You must have complete concentration, which is far more difficult than determination, and you must also have the will to continue, the patience and the faith. These are the vital ingredients. The mailed-fist-determined-to-conquer-the-world approach will not work, and certainly it will never please, in playing the violin. Attitudes which are arbitrary, interpretations which are forced, even determined attitudes about the career, all injure the quality of the playing. It could be summed up by saying that brutality has no place in the life of the violin.

Static truth decays. All truths must be refined and adapted with each use and application; truths of music as well as life-truths. There is a German expression which says that 'Of two contestants it is the thinking one who wins.' When the child learns the instrument he has on his side that great boon: unlimited time. As one grows older, time diminishes and one has to work with precision, economy and commitment in order to achieve work of quality within a minimum amount of time. By analysis and cool development of subtle sensa-

145

tions I find that I have improved the quality of my sound, reduced tension, acquired greater precision and expression of pitch, liberated my musical inspiration and worked less. It is curious but I note that my form, after I have had a week or two of rest, improves as specific tension disappears. However, after a rest of this sort, it is necessary to begin very consciously to win my way back to the standard of playing I aim for, while at the same time without trying too hard, without trying really to play before the muscles and nerves are ready for this. To be able to work quietly and without strain and not to push oneself beyond feelings of mild tiredness has taken me a long time to learn. It is a wonderful sense of release from dead, blind, drudgery to know that it is possible in a quiet, delightful and satisfying way to achieve better form, better direction, with less effort.

Life holds an extraordinary number of pitfalls and challenges. I think probably it does no good to rush forward. Certainly, in the case of the violinist, it is a mistake to take the bull by the horns. For we are not matadors. And when you think of it, the matador does not train except through concentration, grace, precision, alertness, timing and coordination. In fact, the matador must learn everything that applies equally to instrumental playing. It is almost as if with an artist one begins life with a certain amount of talent and a degree of determination. The aim is to achieve wisdom and action with ease. That is not easy but it is possible.

The violinist must learn to control every possible shade of harmonic colour. He must be able to play with a wide, a fat, a slow, a narrow vibrato; he must learn to play with every kind of vibrato right down to no vibrato

146

at all. The aim of these exercises, attitudes and approaches is to make all roads clear. When we have polished and smoothed out an exercise, when we have the various joints in the whole body working, when the avenues are open to expression, then emotion takes over, then intellect, and the two joined guide the musician directly. There is the further question of whether the musician knows what he or she wants to hear. But by preparing the palette the good musician will soon come to learn how to use it. It is possible that it might be used with considerable lack of style, which happens when a performer is not aware of the true nature of the composition. But what is important is the readiness to express oneself, and that can happen only when all the avenues are clear. It is perfectly possible, and examples are legion, for violinists who have defects in their playing still to convey everything they wish. It particularly happens with people who are possessed with the need to play and will overcome naturally what deficiencies they have. Indeed, sometimes these deficiencies may contribute to the good character of their performance. We must not overlook the fact that everyone is different and that sometimes it is the very fighting against difficulties which gives conviction and power to a performance.

The process of violin playing must be controlled by the instinct which is working on thoroughly prepared material. The material has to be refined in advance so that it will accept the instinctive response which you bring to it. It is rather like the wind blowing through a tree. It is the lie of the leaves, each at their own unique angle, that gives a particular voice to the wind.

As I finish this chapter of my 'life-long' class, this must be the moment to confess, to myself and to the reader, frailty, feebleness and fault; to admit to many errors of judgment and action, and to caution my readers against blind acceptance, submission without question. I advocate that in the handling of any problem in life one should aim for a balance, remaining sensitively responsive, analytical and pragmatic, with an attitude both critical and encouraging. I dedicate my book to all my colleagues, young and old, in the hope that I may spare them time and trouble (though not effort and thought) and that they may thus be allowed to give and receive joy and wisdom, support and help in more abundant measure.